Say Goodbye *to* Shame

and 77 Other Stories of Hope and Encouragement *for* a *Lady in Waiting*

SAY GOODBYE *to* SHAME

and 77 OTHER STORIES OF HOPE AND ENCOURAGEMENT *for* A *LADY IN WAITING*

BY

JACKIE KENDALL

BEST-SELLING AUTHOR OF LADY IN WAITING

Take note that the name satan and related names are not capitalized. We choose not to acknowledge him, even to the point of violating grammatical rules.

Destiny Image® Publishers, Inc.
P.O. Box 310
Shippensburg, PA 17257-0310

"Speaking to the Purposes of God for This Generation
and for the Generations to Come"

ISBN 0-7684-2161-6

(Previously published under ISBN 1-56043-306-X)

For Worldwide Distribution
Printed in the U.S.A.

1 2 3 4 5 6 7 8 9 / 09 08 07 06 05 04

This book and all other Destiny Image, Revival Press, MercyPlace, Fresh Bread, Destiny Image Fiction, and Treasure House books are available at Christian bookstores and distributors worldwide.

For a U.S. bookstore nearest you, call
1-800-722-6774.
For more information on foreign distributors, call
717-532-3040.
Or reach us on the Internet:
www.destinyimage.com

Dedication

Dedicated to my wonderful husband, Ken, our great kids, Ben and Jessica, and my tirelessly faithful ministry partner and friend, DeDe Kendall.

Acknowledgments

Special thanks to Susan Fonger for her invaluable contribution to these glimpses of my heart in print.

Thanks to my talented editorial team: Colleen Davidson, Susan Fonger, Daniel Dodds, GeorgiAna Larson, Jamie Puckett, Cheryl Stults, and Linda and Virginia Wells and to my encouraging reading team: Christine, DeDe, Kimberly, LeeAnn, Michele, Ruth, Sandy, and Mom.

Special thanks to Tim and Christine Burke, whose financial sacrifice turned a dream into a reality.

Special salute to Linda Wells (Wellsy) for her labor of love. Her enthusiasm never subsided from the first rough draft to the final submission of the manuscript.

Special, special, special thanks to my threesome (Ken, Ben, and Jessica) who were patient while I wrote and rewrote and rewrote this book.

ENDORSEMENTS

"...Be the first in your neighborhood to try *Say Good-bye to Shame.* I have no doubt you will start a fad."

—Jan Silvious
Author, Conference Speaker, Broadcaster

"Jackie has a unique ability to bring to life Biblical insights which are derived from heart-wrenching personal experience and a deep passion for God. In *Say Good-bye to Shame,* this contagious passion is communicated in a creative manner that draws you closer to the God you can trust in every situation."

—Dr. Elizabeth Francisco
Assistant Professor of Psychology
Trinity College at Miami

"I was deeply moved and challenged by the writings in this book. As I reached the end of the book, I realized that these were not just a set of good teachings, but the reflections of a woman whose foremost passion in life is Jesus Christ."

—Cheryl L. M. Stults, Ph.D.
Assistant Research Professor
San Francisco State University

Contents

Crime—Keeping Good News to Oneself

On April 15, 1967, at a teen Bible study, Larry Munos showed me how I could receive the gift of eternal life. I couldn't resist such a gift! After I left the Bible study, I hurried home to call my best friend. When she answered the phone, I enthusiastically began to tell her how she could receive the gift of eternal life through Jesus Christ. Her response was, "Oh, I already did that when I was in elementary school."

I immediately said, "I probably am not explaining this clearly. I asked Jesus Christ to come into my heart today, and I know I am going to Heaven."

Judy answered in an aggravated voice, "Jackie, I told you I already asked Jesus into my heart when I was at a church camp."

I said, "There is no way you could have such a great gift and not tell me—we've been best friends for two years." We started to argue, and I kept repeating how shocked I was that my best friend could have kept secret something so significant as *knowing how to get to Heaven.* I remember getting off the phone and praying that I would never be the kind of Christian who would keep such good news a secret.

For many years now, I have met Christians who, like my best friend, are comfortable with keeping this good news to themselves. I have always felt it is a crime to keep such good news from those who are needy. I found a story in the Old Testament that verifies my feelings concerning this crime.

In Second Kings 6:24–7:20, famine had overcome the city of Samaria. The desperate condition was reflected in an incident where a mother proposed that parents eat one another's children. Four lepers from this needy city realized they would find no relief for their desperate condition. Men who lived daily with physical and emotional stress, these four lepers left the city of no hope and "happened" upon a campsite that apparently had been abandoned by the enemy. They found horses and donkeys and tents full of food, silver, gold, and clothing. As they were eating and celebrating their great fortune, the four lepers simultaneously said to one another, "Hey, this ain't right!!" (*ain't—appropriate jargon for lepers who have been kept out of the better schools in Israel*). Four desperate men understood that their good fortune was not for their needs alone but for sharing with other needy people. Their leprosy could have convinced them of their justified selfishness, but their non-leprous hearts showed them the crime of keeping good news to oneself.

> *...We're not doing right. This is a day of good news and we are keeping it to ourselves. If we wait until daylight, punishment will overtake us. Let's go at once and report this to the royal palace* (2 Kings 7:9).

REFLECTION...

____

____

____

____

____

____

____

____

____

____

____

____

____

THE PRO AND I

The first movie I remember seeing as a child was *The King and I.* I was only in the third grade, but I was captivated by the film as I sat in that theater with my grandmother. Thirty years later, I saw Yul Bryner in a stage production of the movie; I was again captivated, much as I had been as a child.

As a teenager, I was similarly captivated, not by a movie or movie star but by the love of a big retired NFL pro who turned his back on the screaming fans of the NFL to give his energy to a less impressive audience—searching teens. Week after week, that big football player would tackle the challenges of trying to reach teenagers in the public high schools of San Diego. Once Ray "tackled" a teen, he would hold that teen captive week by week in a wonderful Bible study that he led. I had the privilege of attending that home Bible study. That former NFL football player helped lay the original foundation for my walk with Jesus. He taught me as a teen how to not just believe in Jesus, but how to rely totally upon Jesus moment by moment.

Ray never knew about the dysfunctional home that I came from. I was too ashamed to ever share such private pain. He never knew the fear that I often lived with at night regarding my father. But he did know the most invaluable truth—that Jesus is the only One who will ever satisfy my hungry heart. Ray pushed me and several other teens to get into the Word of God daily to search for the answers to our many questions.

Recently I spoke to retired NFL athletes who were conducting high school assemblies as part of an effort to reach teens. I told them about the "Pro and I" and how to this day Ray has no idea what happened to that teenager whom he used to call "Jack the Quack." How shocked he would be if he knew how much Jesus has used me during the last 30 years! I think about the adults who financially supported Ray's ministry, which helped my life and the lives of other teens. Those adults may not know until eternity what their investment produced for the glory of Jesus.

Do you ever feel like you give and give and your work is just in vain? Do you ever feel like your efforts are fruitless? Do you ever consider quitting? Does the time and money that you have given as a Christian seem to be a good investment? Often I get exhausted and wonder if what I am doing will last beyond the end of the day, much less reach into eternity. Ray *gave* to me without ever seeing any tangible results. I have *given* to many, but I have no idea what they are doing today. A verse that cheers me on when I can't see the eternal results is:

> *And so, brothers of mine, stand firm! Let nothing move you as you busy yourselves in the Lord's work. Be sure that nothing you do for Him is ever lost or ever wasted* (1 Corinthians 15:58 Phillips).

REFLECTION...

A PEARL IN A PILE OF MANURE

As chaplain for my college dorm, I gave devotions on Monday nights. I used personal stories from my painful background as examples. Time and time again, students accused me of "exaggerating or lying." Years later, I realized that most of my audience (preacher/missionary kids, church-grown kids) on those Monday nights were not ready for the crazy family I had grown up with. Once, when I told a college counselor about my family background, she just cried. We both sat in silence for a long time.

One evening before I left for college, a friend of mine came by my parents' house to pick me up and take me out for a farewell dinner. As she waited for me (I was running late as usual), a fight broke out between my dad and youngest brother. It escalated as other family members joined the battle (there were nine in my family). Finally, I was ready to go, and as we were getting in my friend's car, she said something I never forgot. From the mouth of a conservative southern belle came the following, "Jackie, you are like a pearl in a pile of ___________!" At first I was shocked. Then we burst into laughter. Later that night, as I returned to my parents' house, I wondered if God could possibly use someone from such an odorous environment.

In college, I discovered another pearl from an equally unlikely place. This pearl was found in Moab, which is referred to as "God's washbasin." Yet within the dirty rinse water of Moab, God found a pearl named Ruth. He brought that pearl to Bethlehem, and she married a pillar of strength (Boaz). That pearl, found in a washbasin, became part of the lineage of Jesus. She became the mother of Obed, who was the grandfather of King David and the great, great, great...grandfather of Jesus.

I am not in the lineage of Jesus like Ruth, but in 1967 the Pearl of Great Price—Jesus—(see Matt. 13:45-46 KJV) found this pearl (me) in a pile of manure. He not only blessed me with a husband like Boaz, but also with two "godly seeds" (Mal. 2:15 KJV). I wonder if you have to be a pearl snatched from a washbasin or a pile of manure to appreciate all that the Pearl of Great Price does daily for you. I used to be ashamed of the family I came from, but as the years passed, I realized that my family's dysfunction was preparation for a ministry to other pearls from various piles of dysfunction. As a pearl rescued from the pile, I am often so overwhelmed with gratitude that I feel like the following:

> *...Who am I, O Sovereign LORD, and what is my family, that you have brought me this far?...Is this your usual way of dealing with man...?* (2 Samuel 7:18-19)

Reflection...

____

____

____

____

____

____

____

____

____

____

____

____

____

____

CAUTIOUS IN FRIENDSHIP

In 1969, a Campus Life leader was giving me a ride to a teen Bible study. As we rode along in her VW bug, I noticed a sticker on her dashboard: "As one associates, one becomes." I asked her about the quote and she said, "Jackie, you will become like those you spend the most time associating with. Your friends are shaping you and your future." I was a new Christian and still trying to hang on to my non-Christian friends, which was causing such inward conflict. That little chat in the VW bug has influenced me throughout my whole Christian life. I have watched my walk with God become lukewarm and my zeal diminish as I spent too many hours with mediocre, apathetic Christians. I have also noticed that my hunger for Jesus increases after spending time with passionate followers of Jesus. "A righteous man is cautious in friendship" (Prov. 12:26a).

When I was 20 years old, my closest friend was 30 years older than I was. For two years, I spent every possible free moment with Mamie. She taught me how to study and to teach God's Word. She had a passion for God that I had never seen before, and I wanted to know Jesus as intimately as she did. We were like Elijah and Elisha. I was always praying for a "double portion" of the power I saw manifested in Mamie's life. I was often teased during that time for spending so much time with a woman who could be my mother. I was motivated by the reality of following her as she followed Jesus.

When I went away to a Christian college, the Lord gave me another passionate woman of God (31 years older), and through our friendship I learned that Jesus would take all the hurts that had touched my life and bring good from each painful blow (see 2 Cor. 1:3-5). The Lord took her to heaven the year I left college.

Friendships often develop because of common goals and ideals: job relating, parenting concerns, school involvement, children's sports programs, church fellowship/ministries, and community affairs. Can two walk together, except they are agreed? (see Amos 3:3) The friendships in my life that have lasted through all the different stages, dreams, and goals have been the friendships where Jesus was our constant common goal and ideal.

Think about the people with whom you spend the most time, and consider the characteristics that are shaping their lives and yours. Are some of your friends like the one described in Steven Curtis Chapman's song, "Walk With the Wise"? Do you have friends wiser than you? Do you have friends more mature than you?

He who walks with the wise grows wise (Proverbs 13:20a).

REFLECTION...

THE SPIRITUALLY ELITE

When I was a senior in high school, Al Kinard came to town. He began teaching at some of the local Bible studies in San Diego, and he became a buzzword connected to "The Spiritually Elite." I was only a year old in Jesus. I must confess that I was one who was "zealous for God, but their [my] zeal is [was] not based on knowledge" (see Rom. 10:2). When I first heard him speak, Al talked about having power to live victoriously. As a struggling new believer, I found this message very appealing.

I heard him speak several times—he began to talk about leaving San Diego for a farm in Fresno where people could come and live if they "really wanted to live wholeheartedly for Jesus." This was the '60s, so communes were popular in California; I figured this was going to be a Christian commune. Al invited all of us to come if we "really wanted to follow Jesus."

To go with Al, there were *rules* to be followed:

1. We had to leave our families behind, leaving secretly.

2. We could only wear white muslin clothing to all meetings. (We could keep our jeans for the farm work!)

3. We could only bring our Bible, and any money we could donate to the common purse would be shared.

So, five friends and I ran away to "follow Jesus." Of course, our families were frantic and the search began. In retrospect, here were six teenagers wanting to win their families to Jesus, and their choices were having the complete opposite effect—our parents thought we had lost our minds.

One morning at the commune, I overheard a very harsh conversation between Al (our holy leader) and a young teenage girl. He spoke so abusively that when I went up on the roof (literally) to pray, Jesus spoke so softly and said, "Jackie, would I ever speak to a young person in the manner that Al did?" Wow, with that one question the light went on; I knew we had been deceived and we needed to escape this commune.

I devised a middle-of-the-night departure. We knew we did not have the courage to try to leave this "elite group" in broad daylight. We knew they would try to "guilt" us into staying by challenging our commitment to Jesus. They had already said that our leaving would only prove we were not of the "true flock," that we were goats and not sheep. The six of us returned to San Diego, and before we went home, we spent a whole day praying and fasting (no money for food—just enough for gas to get home). Jesus gave us a verse to teach us that "spiritual eliteness" is too often deep deception and distraction from focusing on ***Jesus***.

> *But I am afraid that just as Eve was deceived by the serpent's cunning, your minds may somehow be led astray from your sincere and pure devotion to Christ* (2 Corinthians 11:3).

Reflection...

___

___

___

___

___

___

___

___

___

___

A Scholarship on a Silver Tray

Going to college was never up for discussion in our home: Surviving day to day and finishing high school were major accomplishments. In fact, I was the only one of seven children who did not drop out of high school. So, graduating from college would be like getting a doctorate in our family. After high school, I got a job as a church secretary and started taking a few courses at the local community college. I loved my job at the church because of the ministry that I was able to have with young people even though I was just a secretary.

Throughout the two years that I worked at the church, whenever I would speak, the pastors and adults always asked me what college I was going to attend. When I would tell them about my job at the church, they would always say, "You need to get your college degree." Their comments often bugged me, and I prayed about my desire to go to a Christian college—knowing full well that such a desire was an impossible dream. I was making $72 a week, and my parents didn't have a dime to spare, especially for a Christian college.

Whenever I would remark about praying for money to go to a Christian college, my father would sarcastically reply: "Do you think God is going to drop a silver tray with money on it out of heaven?" I would just grin and pray even harder.

A rich elderly couple heard me speak one Sunday afternoon, and the Lord allowed me to find such favor with them! They were so impressed with my zeal for the Lord that they offered to pay for me to go with Campus Crusade to Spain for a special evangelistic campaign. I wrote to ask them to consider a long-term investment in my life. I asked if they would consider giving me the designated funds for college rather than a trip to Spain for two weeks. Mr. Turner was a little put out by my candid request, but Florence, his wife, prayed about it. Mrs. Turner tried to contact me, but I was counseling and teaching at youth camp. After returning from camp, I was invited to dinner at their penthouse condo in Palm Beach.

That evening they told me that God had put on Epa's (Florence's) heart the desire to send me to college. This desire not only included tuition, room, and board, but also a monthly expense account that would cover my airplane flights home, long distance phone calls, clothing, and pizza. I was so stunned that my junker car and I almost did not make it home. I could hardly concentrate on the road in front of me because of the "silver tray" that was holding my full scholarship for college.

Years later, the Lord polished this silver tray when I found out that I am the only young person (outside of immediate family) to whom such a scholarship has ever been given. I am still flabbergasted, though it is more than 25 years later!

> *How can I repay the LORD for all his goodness to me?*
> *(Psalm 116:12)*

REFLECTION...

___

___

___

___

___

___

___

___

___

___

___

GOD'S NEW CREATURE PROGRAM

An annual event for the college I attended was a sweetheart banquet and the choosing of a sweetheart queen. During my freshman year, my gown went to this banquet, but I was not wearing it. In fact, my clothes had more dates in my freshman year than I ever did. I was not popular with the guys, but my clothes sure were with my dormmates; my closet was like a costume rental shop.

To my total surprise, I was nominated to run for sweetheart queen my second year at college. The competition was based not only on our external appearance, but also on the degree that we inwardly reflected the ideals of this Christian college. Each candidate had to go before the whole student body (4,000) and tell how Jesus had made a difference in her life.

Giving my testimony in front of 4,000 people was not intimidating to me. I had been only six months old in the Lord when I was given the privilege of giving my testimony at the San Diego Civic Auditorium in front of 5,000 people. What was intimidating in this situation was the candidates with whom I would be competing; every candidate was either a preacher's kid, a missionary's kid, or a professor's kid. I was just a kid from a very ungodly home. I was convinced that my "bad" upbringing would ultimately disqualify me. In fact, when we were practicing for the night of the banquet, I paid close attention to the part concerning *how to exit the stage when the winner was announced.* I assumed that I would be one of the girls to exit the stage.

Does it sound like I was very insecure in college? Ironically, my insecurity was fueled regularly by someone who works 24 hours a day to challenge the righteousness of any Christian. "For the accuser [satan the shamer] of our brothers, who accuses them before our God day and night, has been hurled down" (Rev. 12:10b). Whenever I would hear details of the loving Christian homes in which the various students were raised, I would be filled with shame concerning the home I came from—shame, not from God, but from the accuser.

When they announced the winner on the night of the banquet, the first picture taken of the queen captured her eyes looking toward the exit stairway. Yes, I won! And, the accuser showed up on stage for a moment. They put the crown on my head; my escort (my future husband) walked me to the throne and placed roses in my arms. All the while, the accuser whispered in my ear: "If they knew what I know about your past, you never would have won." I was caught off guard for only a moment. Then King Jesus reminded me of my enrollment in His "New Creature Program."

For too many years, I listened to the accuser while he used my past and my ungodly family to shame me. One day the Lord showed me that my painful family origin helped prepare the very platform from which I speak boldly today.

> *Therefore, if anyone is in Christ, he is a new creation; the old has gone, the new has come!* (2 Corinthians 5:17)

Reflection...

____

____

____

____

____

____

____

____

____

MAY I BORROW YOUR BODY?

A college roommate borrowed my favorite dress for a very special date. That date turned out to be the night she became engaged. One night during her first year of marriage, she and her husband were dressing for another special date. Her husband asked her to wear his favorite dress. When she asked him what dress he was referring to, he told her it was the dress she had worn on the night they were engaged. She grinned and said that she needed to call Jackie because she had borrowed the dress from me.

Borrowing is not a new concept. Borrowing is limitless. People borrow almost anything: lawn equipment, tools, cars, money, even wedding gowns. (My wedding gown was borrowed by three other women.)

Jesus borrowed a human body so He could leave heaven, walk among men, and ultimately offer redemption to all mankind. This borrowing of a human body has a sophisticated theological term, *incarnation.* One day I was thinking about the body in which Jesus was willing to be confined as He walked on this earth. Jesus was able to do the will of the Father in a human body; I realized that I can do the will of the Father in *my* human body. Then, I realized what Paul's reference to the Christian's body being a temple where the Holy Spirit dwells (see 1 Cor. 6:19) really means: It validates that God intends to use my body for His purpose. My free will determines whether I let Him borrow my body today for His will. Doing the will of the Father is allowing *my body to be borrowed by the Holy Spirit to expedite the will of the Father here on earth.* Jesus was incarnated 2,000 years ago; this incarnation process continues in the "borrowed" bodies of His followers.

Knowing that God is borrowing my body gives me confidence whenever I get a chance to do the will of the Father. Whether I am sharing Christ with a stranger on a plane or in the grocery store, whether I am teaching 5 women or 500—all these opportunities are just another chance for the Spirit of God to borrow my body as a heavenly microphone on this planet. The Spirit of God wants to borrow your body to finish the will of your Father.

Consider the irony of a Christian being thrilled to have Jesus purchase her body with His blood so she may go to heaven, but this same person resists God's desire to borrow her body to accomplish His work here on earth. He purchased us with His blood, but our free will still places our bodies in our control. So, if God is going to borrow my body to speak or minister to someone on this planet, I must be willing to loan my body to Him. Paul felt that loaning my body to God on a continual basis was my "reasonable service." When you let Him borrow your body, you will be thrilled with the things He does with such a frail human frame. "Excuse me, may I borrow your body?" Body borrowed by Jesus...cool, huh?

> *...I beg you, my brothers, as an act of intelligent worship, to give Him your bodies...* (Romans 12:1 Phillips).

REFLECTION...

____

____

____

____

____

____

____

____

____

____

____

The Message at the Red Light

When I graduated from high school, I started to date a wonderful Christian guy (the first Christian I ever dated) who was on staff with Youth for Christ. Our dating relationship seemed to be the talk of the town—and this was no small town—San Diego. We consciously sought the Lord concerning His blueprints for dating, and we enjoyed not only one another but also the Lord together. What could be better??? Then my parents moved to Florida, so I made arrangements to continue to live in San Diego—of course, I did not want to move some 3,000 miles away from the man of my dreams.

A year later, returning from a big Youth for Christ rally, David said he needed to talk with me. As he began to talk, I sensed that he was having difficulty with what he was trying to tell me. When he finally blurted out, "The Lord wants me to break up with you," I was so shocked that I just burst out crying. His response to my tears was, "Where is your faith—why are you crying so hard?"

Shocked at his judgmental remark, I was stunned into silence. Then I blurted out, "Faith does not put sand bags in front of a person's tear ducts." He made a few more comments and then got out of the car and went into his parents' home.

As I drove away from his house, I stopped at a red light. I think that I sat there through several lights (it was after midnight so there was no traffic behind my car). When I finally noticed that the light turned red again, the red light was magnified in the darkness, and it suddenly made me think of the blood of Jesus. A verse I had just memorized came to my mind: "He that spared not his own Son, but delivered him up for us all, how shall he not with him also freely give us all things?" (see Rom. 8:32 KJV) Talk about a moment of truth—if God gave up the best for me, then with the best—Jesus—He will give me what is best for me. When I allowed myself to think that my Mr. Wonderful was not God's best for me, I actually began to smile as I tried to imagine someone who would possibly be better for me than my David. As the light turned green, I drove home to my little rented room with a peace and joy that passed all understanding—knowing that God had only the best in mind not only for me, but also for David. Two years later he married a nurse who can care for him, for he now has multiple sclerosis.

Time and time and time again, I have been able to encourage others with the reality of Romans 8:32. I have watched God prove Himself to those who would dare to believe that life is worth living when life was not on their terms but on God's terms! Oh, the terrible burden to always want life on our terms! What a secure place awaits the woman who has finally surrendered the terrible burden of not trusting that God's blueprints are God's best for her.

> *He who did not grudge His own Son but gave Him up for us all—can we not trust such a God to give us, with Him, everything else that we can need?* (Romans 8:32 Phillips)

REFLECTION...

____

____

____

____

____

____

____

____

____

____

OVERCHARGED BY WORRY

This morning while studying I came across the following warning from Jesus:

> *Be careful, or your hearts will be weighed down with dissipation, drunkenness and the anxieties of life, and that day will close on you unexpectedly like a trap* (Luke 21:34).

> *Watch out! Don't let me find you living in* ***careless ease*** *and* ***drunkenness****, and filled with the* ***worries of this life****. Don't let that day catch you unaware, as in a trap...* (Luke 21:34-35 NLT).

What do I need to watch out for?

1. Careless ease (Greek): Refers to a **headache** from over-indulgence.

How often do we **overindulge** on this life and wake up with morning hangovers from being more stuffed by the things of this world than from a feast at the King's table?

2. Drunkenness: As a believer I have never found this to be an issue that would distract me from being ready for my coming bridegroom, or so I thought.

3.Worries of this life (Greek): Lesser things of this life.

As I reflected on drunkenness being a **non-issue**, the Lord pricked my heart with this question: "How often, Jackie, have you been intoxicated by **worry**?" Ouch—that hurt. How often does my day begin like an alcoholic who must have a drink before breakfast, except that my drink of choice is the **wine of worry**??? How often have I had a tall glass of Foaming Worry before going to bed? How often have my family members seen me distracted by intoxicating worries about **lesser things**, *temporal things*? How often have those I loved suffered the consequences of **my heart being weighed down by worry**? How often have I had to take Advil for a hangover from stress?

The worst aspect of this intoxication is that it is the opposite of trust.

> *"Because he loves me," says the Lord, "I will rescue him; I will protect him, for he acknowledges my name. He will call upon me, and I will answer him ..."* (Ps. 91:14-15).

As I continued to ponder intoxicating worry, I decided to look up the King James version of Luke 21:34. I gasped when I saw this phrase: "And take heed to yourselves, lest at any time your hearts be overcharged with surfeiting, and drunkenness, and cares of this life...."

Wow, ***worry overcharges my heart***. Worry demands more than my heart was ever intended to give (or function, or perform).

Let's begin today by resisting that first glass of the wine of worry. Let's switch to a ***tall glass of living water***. I may have to start a new chapter of AA—AA for worriers who want to be delivered from overcharged, weighed down, burdened and intoxicated hearts. If we take this exhortation seriously, then our Bridegroom will not have to compete with our worry headaches and hangovers. Our heavenly Bridegroom is the One who spoke this warning. I have not always been a good listener when my husband warns me about particular people or activities, and I have lived with the consequences. Today I want to stop being ***overcharged*** by worry so that both my earthly bridegroom and my heavenly Bridegroom do not have to handle a woman drunk on worry and stress.

> *An anxious heart weighs a man down...* (Prov. 12:25).

REFLECTION...

____

____

A HUMAN SPARKLER

As a group of elected people, Israel had been chosen by God to glorify Him, but they failed miserably. I was deeply moved as I read about this in Dwight Edwards's book, *Revolution Within.*[1] The author's insights pulled at my heartstrings: Israel failed in their purpose because they *profaned* God's name! When I think about what *profane* means, I think of "blasphemy" and "sacrilege." Edwards explained that *profane* also means "common."

Ezekiel 36:20 says, "And wherever they went among the nations, they profaned my holy name...."

I looked up *profaned* and, sure enough, in Hebrew it means "to blaspheme," "to curse," and "common." The dictionary definition of the word common is "ordinary, mediocre, humdrum, cheap, colorless, dull, drab."

Wow, all of us *profane* God's name when we represent Him as common, ordinary, dull in our lives. When we do not allow God to sparkle and shine through us, then our extraordinary, awesome God appears common and ordinary to those around us. Yikes! I mourn for our incomparable God who is daily *profaned* in our lives.

When we tremble in the midst of a crisis; when we are anxious, full of doubt; when we show fear; or when we fret, we relegate our God to a position of mediocrity, to ordinariness. When we display these attitudes, we display to others that our God is not big enough to handle our problems, not powerful enough. If He is as incomparable as the Word declares, then we should not be anything but confident in a trustworthy God and His infinite grace.

I have spent hours examining the areas of my life where I don't allow God to shine and sparkle through me. If I want to glorify God, then I need to allow

1. Dwight is a descendent of Jonathan Edwards.

my life to be a display of *His extraordinary capacity*—only then is He glorified and only then do I become a "Human Sparkler."

My prayer today is that I will allow God to sparkle through the display window. I do not want to insult Him by allowing those around me to think I love and serve a common, ordinary, mediocre, dull, or colorless Sovereign.

A popular phrase among youth leaders is, "We are here to make God look good." Kay Author captures this thought in her book *To Know Him by Name.* She writes, "You are to live in such a way as to give all of creation a correct opinion or estimate of who God is." (p.18, Questar Publishers, Inc. Sisters, Oregon, 1995)

A "Human Sparkler" is the best case in defense of an incomparable, extraordinary God!

> *And all of us have had that veil removed so that we can be mirrors that brightly reflect the glory of the LORD...* (2 Corinthians 3:18 NLT)

REFLECTION...

____

____

____

____

____

____

____

____

____

____

____

I BELIEVED A LIE

I was standing on the platform as the matron of honor for a precious young friend whom I had loved and spiritually discipled for several years. As her bridegroom began to say his vows, he began to weep. His best man (his father) began to cry. I did not cry—I sobbed. What people in the audience did not know was the cause of my deep sobbing. Many had assumed that my tears were from the joy of seeing Christina and Michael unite in Christ. I may have begun crying for that reason initially, but the tears of joy turned to painful sobbing after the father of lies whispered: "Your bridegroom did not weep for you because you were damaged goods."

That one lie turned into hundreds of thoughts that spiraled around the lie—thoughts like: *God gave Christina a wonderful Christian home to grow up in, with two loving parents and two great brothers. She grew up in a home where laughter and music were a common occurrence. I, in contrast, grew up in a non-Christian, abusive home, where screaming, fighting, and verbal abuse were the music I heard daily. I was not given the blessings that Christina had. And, yes, I was damaged goods on my wedding day.*

From one little lie, I spiraled into a deep ditch of self-pity. Jesus saw the self-pity ditch that I had fallen into, and the next day He showed me that my heavenly Bridegroom has wept for me. He wept in the garden and bravely faced the Cross because of the joy that was set before Him—the joy of offering me forgiveness and taking me as His bride. He even gave me the Holy Spirit as my engagement ring (see Eph. 1:13). Jesus is madly in love with me (see Eph. 3:18). I had a choice to make: Believe Jesus or believe the father of lies.

You may be wondering by now: *How can a Christian who has the Spirit of Truth within her believe such a lie?* You may wonder how I could believe a lie when I am a follower of the truth. Let me try to explain. Daily I have the choice to either believe the truth or to exchange the *truth* for a lie. I have the choice to wound myself through lies or to be healed through truths.

Adam and Eve were in a perfect relationship with God Almighty, but that perfect relationship did not keep Eve from believing a lie. We must recognize that as Christians we are following the truth, studying the truth, and living the truth, but that does not immunize us, as believers, from being exposed to lies and even choosing to believe lies. We have a legacy of lies because we were originally followers of the father of lies (see Jn. 8:44). Airwaves are overflowing with lies from the prince of the power of the air (see Eph. 2:2).

Have you been telling yourself the truth? If so, you are enroute to emotional health. If you've been telling yourself lies, then you struggle regularly with guilt and feelings of never measuring up.

> *Then you will know the truth, and the truth will set you free* (John 8:32).

REFLECTION...

____

____

____

____

____

____

____

____

____

____

____

ARE YOU GUILTY OF ACHAN'S SIN?

In a familiar story, the reader could miss an obvious nugget. Reading through Joshua, I came upon the story of Achan and his sin of craving the beautiful Babylonian robe, the silver coins, and the bar of gold. Many know the story of how he took these items and hid them in his tent. That was a sin because it directly violated God's instruction concerning the conquering of Jericho (see Josh. 6:18-19). When I reread this familiar story I was focusing on the lust that drove Achan to disobey and the costly cravings that resulted in the deaths of himself and his family. This deadly craving reminded me of the many addictions that destroy so many American homes. Then the Lord rocked my world by revealing to me another aspect of the tragedy. I had assumed Achan's sin was lust, but it was the deeper sin of presumption.

When God gave the marching orders for Jericho, He said, "No plunder for the warriors." Being a warrior, Achan heard that instruction and proceeded to commit a "presumptuous sin." He ***assumed*** that the "no plunder for the warriors" would be the marching orders for all the cities they would conquer. So Achan gave in to his lust and cravings. He ***assumed*** that God would not provide for him as a warrior. Sadly, Achan stole in Jericho what God was going to ***freely give him*** in the next city of Ai.

When God gave Joshua the marching orders for Ai, the Lord included, "Keep the captured goods and the cattle for yourselves"(see Josh. 8:2). So Achan's ultimate sin was not only lust, but also the presumption that God would not provide for him as a warrior. **Achan stole what God would have given him if Achan had only trusted El Elyon's timing and specific marching orders.**

> How often do we steal ***too early*** what God ***later*** wants to give us freely?

- How often do we impatiently pursue what our Father wants to give us when we are sitting still? (see Isa. 64:4)

- How often do we panic and conclude that God is not going to provide? (see Matt. 6:25-33)

- How often do we assume what God is going to do next and we rush ahead, drenched in fear that it is not going to be the best for us? (see Rom. 8:32)

- How many times have you and I suffered because we ***assumed*** what God would do and then we were knocked down by the surprise turn of events? (see Isa. 55:8-9)

"Lord, forgive me for a propensity to sin like Achan... Forgive me for living even a moment of my life drenched in fear rather than drenched in faith."

> *This is what the LORD, the Creator and Holy One of Israel, says: "Do you question what I do? Do you give me orders about the work of my hands?"* (Isaiah 45:11 NLT)

REFLECTION...

____

____

____

____

____

____

____

____

____

HOLDING HANDS AFTER ALL THESE YEARS

When I was in college, I was very impressed by the love relationship between my English literature teacher (Dr. Evangeline Banta) and her husband. She invited me to spend a weekend at her home where I got a closer look at a love relationship that I had assumed only existed in literature. At the end of our weekend together, I asked Evangeline what was the secret of their love that had flourished and not shriveled after 40-plus years of marriage. I never forgot her remark, and it has been the most important marital advice I ever received. Evangeline said, "We made a commitment on our wedding night that we would not go to sleep angry with one another." This is such a simple remark, but such a foundational truth for love that will last a lifetime.

Jesus chose the marriage relationship to be a reflection of the heavenly Bridegroom and his earthly Bride. "The marriage relationship is a great mystery, but I see it as a symbol of the marriage of Christ and his Church" (Eph. 5:32 Phillips). I used to cringe when I heard the symbol of marriage compared with Christ and His Church since so many marriages are in such pitiful conditions today.

Then I realized that the emotional divorce in most marriages—caused by unresolved conflict (too many nights going to bed angry)—is the same emotional divorce I see between Christ and His Church. So many Christians are divorced from true intimacy with God because the Holy Spirit has been grieved (see Eph. 4:30) and quenched (see 1 Thess. 5:19 KJV). Ironically, the Holy Spirit is "grieved" by a separation, a gap, when we do not willingly put away anger and bitterness (see Eph. 4:31).

Our natural marriage relationship experiences the same gaps and grief when we do not deal with our anger and bitterness. Just as Christians can choose to live with a gap between God and themselves, many couples choose to live day in and day out with gaps as wide as the English Channel.

At my bridal shower, married women were encouraged to give me advice, which was recorded for me by the hostess of the shower. Every married woman gave her version of the advice that Evangeline gave me that weekend. One woman challenged me to be the first one to make the move across the emotional Grand Canyon caused by conflict. Men are so uncomfortable with emotional realities and need marriage to teach them about handling anger before the sun sets daily. This same woman said that the "first move" in resolving conflict is the most difficult moment, but once the first step is taken, one senses the ability to sprint into the rest of the process. Pouting renders one unable to walk, much less sprint into conflict resolution.

I have often been grateful for the days when the sun shines for a longer period—I feel as though that day is a bonus day in resolving conflict before the sun sets.

> *If you are angry, be sure that it is not a sinful anger. Never go to bed angry—don't give the devil that sort of foothold* (Ephesians 4:26-27 Phillips).

REFLECTION...

THE ULTIMATE SEDUCTION

When I fast, my time in God's Word is often quite sensitive and illuminating. One morning, the following verse caught my attention: "Satan rose up against Israel and incited David to take a census of Israel" (1 Chron. 21:1). Satan incited David. What does *incited* mean? I looked up *incited* in my Strong's concordance and found that incited comes from the words: "stimulate, seduce." Satan seduced David to count the military. What was wrong with counting the military? Why would satan seduce David to do something that was not a violation of Mosaic law? Why was Joab so repulsed (see 1 Chron. 21:6) by David's command?

What David did was evil in the sight of God (see 1 Chron. 21:7), but I could not see why. I could understand that David's adultery with Bathsheba was sin. I saw his murdering Uriah as a clearly evil move, but what was I missing in this command to count the military of Israel and Judah? Then the Lord turned on the light in my heart. I saw clearly that the evil done by David was not the *census* but the *motive* behind David's actions. David wanted to know how many fighting men in Israel and Judah he could depend on. Joab, as well as God, did not see David's actions as being those of a responsible warrior-king. David's actions were manifestations of "self-reliance" rather than "God-reliance." David's *motive*, which is hidden to the naked eye, was obvious to not only an all-knowing God but also to a discerning friend (Joab).

Joab perceived that David was being seduced to trust in his strength, his army, his past military record. Joab tried to counter the seduction with the statement, "May the Lord multiply his troops a hundred times over" (1 Chron. 21:3a). Joab was challenging David with the fact that the heavenly Commander-in-Chief is an expert at multiplying what we give to Him—whether it is a military army or a mere sack lunch. David did not want to hear

Joab's challenge to his self-trust. Do you have a Joab who will challenge you when you are being seduced to trust in yourself?

David's momentary self-trust cost the death of 70,000 men on whom he had wanted to rely. These soldiers died in a battle between the seducer and one of God's children. Satan, the oldest seducer, began this timeless strategy with Eve, and he continues daily to seduce God's children into trusting themselves more than God.

To trust in myself and others more than Jesus,

To rely on myself and others more than Jesus,

To depend on myself and others more than Jesus,

...is not a mere character flaw, but *sin*. Too often I have dismissed self-reliance as the flaw of an insecure, controlling person. Forgive me, Lord, for allowing this seduction in my life—I want to trust You with my whole heart, soul, and mind.

> ...*You have eaten the fruit of deception. Because you have depended on your own strength and on your many warriors* (Hosea 10:13).

REFLECTION...

Heavenly Potpourri

Good smells, bad smells, stale smells, fresh smells, sweet smells—each of these scents are picked up by our olfactory nerves. Our family consistently uses and overuses the olfactory nervous system—we are a family of "sniffers." Whenever we kiss, we sniff. Whenever we hug, we snatch a sniff. We struggle with the way allergies affect our freedom to sniff and appreciate our environment. When our daughter was young and I would be speaking out of town, she would go into my closet and "sniff" some of my clothes in order to feel my presence.

Did you know that smells, sniffs, and scents are all a biblical reality? Being a "sniffer," I did some research on the different smells/scents in the Bible. I considered the fact that scents are not only given off by people, but also by animals and objects. I discovered three interesting aromas.

I found the obvious scent of animals in the Levitical offerings. Talk about the smell of barbecue on a consistent basis! Whenever the Jews smelled the offerings, they were smelling the scent of a significant relationship with God. The smell of lamb, bull, or goat cooking on the altar (their grill) was a daily reminder to all the "sniffers" that a relationship with the living God is a viable reality.

Objects that give off scents and smells took me to the New Testament where Paul remarked that the gifts he received from other believers were gifts producing an aroma so pleasing to God. The scents from practical gifts (cloak, parchment, food, money) given to Paul were referred to as a heavenly potpourri. "Such generosity is like a lovely fragrance, a sacrifice that pleases the very heart of God" (Phil. 4:18b Phillips). Talk about a new perfume! Celebrities are always having new scents named after them. God's children, through giving, produce new scents on a daily basis. Move over, Liz Taylor! You should smell some of this heavenly potpourri!!

Lastly, I found the most potent heavenly potpourri. This wonderful aroma was from the intimate aspect of people's lives—that is, the intimate privilege of prayer. How awesome to think that my daily prayers are mingled with incense that burns so sweetly before the throne of God—talk about a heavenly moment for any "sniffer"! I can imagine God taking a deep breath, and into His nostrils flows a sweet aroma that comes from the cry of my heart. My prayers may seem so desperate and painful here, but in heaven they are transformed into a heavenly aroma that would thrill any "sniffer"!

> *...He was given much incense to offer, with the prayers of all the saints, on the golden altar before the throne. The smoke of the incense, together with the prayers of the saints, went up before God from the angel's hand* (Revelation 8:3-4).

Reflection...

____

____

____

____

____

____

____

____

____

____

____

____

DIVINE PRAYER ENCOUNTER

> *I urge, then, first of all, that requests, prayers, intercession and thanksgiving be made for everyone* (1 Timothy 2:1).

While separating this verse into bite-sized pieces, I found something new that I had an absolute praise party about. First, the Lord used the expression "first of all" to remind me of the primary role that prayer is to take in my life daily. Secondly, the Lord used the word "everyone" to remind me of the many people that God anticipates my praying for regularly. Then I found the definition of "intercession" and I gasped big time. Intercession has several definitions: "audience with the king," "encounter," "social interaction,"—all of these intimate terms that I love—then I found "chance upon." Now, that phrase my not ring your bell, but it triggered a siren inside of me.

Let me explain. Whenever we take the time to pray, we are positioning ourselves to "chance upon" intimacy with our heavenly Bridegroom. Get this—the phrase "chance upon" radically impacted my life in 1972, when I read Ruth 2:3 where Ruth "chanced upon an encounter" with her future bridegroom. Do you see the connection between "chance upon" and "intercession"? Ruth's "chance encounter" was part of sovereign destiny. Such destiny-filled encounters with our heavenly Bridegroom are available 24/7 to each of us.

When Ruth had her "chance encounter" with her future bridegroom, Boaz spoke encouraging words to her needy heart. When you and I pray, our heavenly Boaz/Bridegroom wants to speak very specific blessings and directions when we "chance upon" such a holy, intimate moment with Him.

We need a more conscious holy pause when we pray, aware that this is an opportunity for "chanced upon" intimacy with our heavenly Bridegroom. Maybe the reason so many of God's people don't hear His voice is this: they know how to beg and implore God with their needs, but they don't expect to hear something specific during their audience with the King! The reality is that most of God's kids know how to pray, but they don't know how to listen. Listening happens in the midst of intimate intercession that is ultimately followed by thanksgiving. Such intimacy with one's heavenly Bridegroom produces a grateful heart that cannot be restrained. This is the sacred romance most people are reading about, yet they are still missing their "chanced upon" intimacy with Jesus.

> *"What other nation is so great as to have their gods near them the way the LORD our God is near us whenever we pray to him?"* (Deuteronomy 4:7)

REFLECTION...

____

____

____

____

____

____

____

____

____

____

____

____

____

____

MOTOR-MOUTH'S HEAVENLY DIARY

When I was only two years old, I was already such a motor-mouth. My mother told me that one evening when they were having a dinner party, I was walking about babbling freely when my father decided I needed to be put in my crib. Will putting a two-year-old in her crib close her lips? Wrong! I actually called out to one of the dinner guests and tried to have a conversation from my crib. I can laugh about the story now, but I have several painful memories of being teased throughout my life concerning the motor that propels my mouth.

When I became a Christian, several of the brethren felt called of God to talk to me about my incessant babbling. They used all the typical verses that exhort a person (especially a woman) to be quiet, like: "study to be quiet" (1 Thess. 4:11 KJV); "quiet and peacable lives" (1 Tim. 2:2); or, "A woman should learn in quietness and full submission" (1 Tim. 2:11). Their favorite verse, with which to shame a "motor-mouth," referred to "the unfading beauty of a gentle and *quiet* spirit, which is of great worth in God's sight" (1 Pet. 3:4). I purchased Strong's Exhaustive Concordance and did a little study on the word *quiet*, especially the use in 1 Pet. 3:4. What a surprise to find that the word "quiet" does not mean sealed lips, but an "undisturbed and peaceful spirit"!

The Book of Proverbs is full of warnings about the misuse and abuse of one's lips and speech. I have always been concerned that I would bless people with my speech and not curse or harm anyone. I also know that where there are many words, the possibility of harmful words exists. I am daily looking to the Holy Spirit to keep a close tab on my speech. I have learned to repent as quickly as He notifies me of my mouth's offense.

In college one evening, I was being teased at the dinner table concerning my "motor-mouth." Just as the shame began to rise in my heart, a young man spoke up and said the neatest phrase this "motor-mouth" had ever heard. He said, "Yeah, she talks a lot, but have you noticed who she talks about incessantly? At least, in all her talking she is saying something worth listening to." A silence fell upon the table. I looked at this young man, smiled, and knew that my "motor-mouth" was being used by the One I loved. That young man eventually became my husband.

Back in my dorm that night, the Lord gave me a verse to remind me how He feels about my incessant chatting with others about Him. Did you know that Jesus listens to the conversations that we have concerning our love for Him, and they are being recorded in a heavenly diary? This "motor-mouth" was liberated that night—for some, that is a blessing, and for others...well, they can buy earplugs at Walgreens.

> *Then those who feared the LORD talked with each other, and the LORD listened and heard. A scroll of remembrance was written in his presence concerning those who feared the LORD and honored his name* (Malachi 3:16).

Reflection...

THE GALATIAN DISEASE

Since 1979, I have been a volunteer nurse working the "Galatian Disease" wing within Christianity. To prepare me for this job, the Lord led me to one of the most legalistic Christian colleges in the United States—a college where I spent four years observing the misery of Christians who live with too little grace and too much emphasis on the letter of the law. "If you try to be justified by the Law you automatically cut yourself off from the power of Christ, you put yourself outside the range of His grace" (Gal. 5:4 Phillips). I spent four years trying to resist becoming infected with the "Galatian Disease."

The "Galatian Disease" has noticeable symptoms: It drains a person of joy and creativity. It fills a person with cynicism. It depletes a person of a loving attitude and replaces it with a judgmental one. This disease-laden individual too often looks like she sucks on lemons on an hourly basis. One of these individuals asked me one day, "Do you sleep with a coat hanger in your mouth so you can smile all day?" Smiling is treated like the ultimate crime. Throughout my four years of training, I almost got my "blesser busted," but I knew how to get immunized against this graceless condition. Whenever I noticed one of the symptoms coming on, I would reread the Book of Galatians and the symptom would subside.

As I tried to stand firm in the freedom that Jesus had won for me (see Gal. 5:1), I was often attacked concerning my emphasis on grace. I was told that my emphasis on grace would give people license to sin (see Gal. 5:13). That caused me legitimate concern; I would never want to encourage anyone to use grace as a passport into sin. Then I realized that anyone who really experiences God's grace does not have the desire to "sin against God" but, on the contrary, that person wants to please the One who called him or her to live as a beneficiary of such amazing grace.

Do legalistic systems motivate Christians to live more holy lives? I have walked with Jesus only 30 years, but I have not observed legalistic Christians as having more success living holy lives than those of us who are motivated and constrained by the grace of God. I honestly believe that God's grace ultimately produces such gratitude in the recipients that the very spring in the steps of their obedience is the spring of grace. I am sure many people take advantage of God's grace, but that is not cured by more laws and rules. I have read many times about God's children taking advantage of God's grace. This particular group of God's kids were in the Old Testament under the strict Mosaic law.

> *Will you steal and murder, commit adultery and perjury, burn incense to Baal and follow other gods you have not known, and then come and stand before me in this house, which bears my Name, and say, "We are safe"—safe to do these detestable things?* (Jeremiah 7:9-10)

Reflection...

____

____

____

____

____

____

____

____

____

____

____

____

BELOVED DOODLES AND I

I went to the post office to pick up a registered letter from our lawyer. Standing in line, I was a little anxious, wondering what the letter was about. I wondered if the IRS had wrapped some red tape around our lawyer, who had been helping us in applying for a non-profit exemption status for Power to Grow Ministry (a ministry that my husband and I had just formed). As I opened the thick envelope, I assumed that more IRS red tape would be enclosed, but I discovered someone's last will and testament. I immediately assumed that Dick's secretary had mailed me the wrong papers. Being a curious female, I began to read the will, and the first interesting thing I read, as I recall, was:

"I direct my Trustee to pay first from income and then from principal, if necessary, the sum of $100 per week to Frieda Houchins, to be used in part for the care of my beloved puppy dog, Doodles, for its lifetime."

As I continued reading, since my attention was captured by Doodles, I came upon the next amazing statement:

"I hereby devise the sum of *Three Thousand Dollars* ($3,000) to Power to Grow, Inc., Jackie Kendall ministries."

Well, I started howling like a puppy, I was so shocked. I did not even know the deceased, yet she had placed me in her will just three and one-half months before her death. Etta Munn had decided to encourage me to continue to give myself with abandon to the Lord she and I both love.

As I drove away from the post office, I started thinking about Etta being with Jesus. Her gift was a way that she could still speak out for Jesus: *though dead, she could still speak*. Etta, like righteous Abel, has offered a pleasing sacrifice to God, a sacrifice whose aroma will continue through the years. Etta put other ministries in her will, enabling many to continue working on earth for the One she is now enjoying face to face.

So beloved Doodles and I are presently being blessed by Etta, who now dwells with Jesus beyond Florida's beautiful blue skies.

> *And by faith he [she] still speaks, even though he [she] is dead* (Hebrews 11:4b).

Reflection...

Everyone Needs Friends Like Daniel's

I was thinking about Daniel, "a man greatly beloved" of God (see Dan. 10:11 KJV). In Hebrew, the word for "beloved" means not only "great delight" and "great desire" but also "delectable." Wow, Daniel's life was actually delectable to God! What amazing favor. Tears filled my eyes because my heart yearned for my own life to be "delectable" to God.

As I looked more closely at Daniel's life, I read about his three friends, and the Lord showed me something truly exciting. We know Daniel's friends as Shadrach, Meshach, and Abednego—the names they were given in captivity in *Babylon.* Their not-so-famous ***Hebrew*** names were Hananiah, Mishael, and Azariah. As I studied the Hebrew translations and meanings of these names, I discovered what kind of friends Daniel had, the kind we all need: friends who want passionately to follow Jesus.

Hananiah means "the Lord is gracious."

Mishael means "the Lord is my help."

Azariah means "Who is like our God?"

Just imagine! Their very names held the messages those friends needed to give one another when all three were cast into the fiery furnace (see Dan. 3). Their names described the gracious, incomparable, helping God who showed up in the furnace as the fourth man. The Lord, who walked in the fiery furnace with them, was the embodiment of all three of their names!!!

Do you have friends who remind you that the Lord is gracious (Jehovah-raah), that He is our helper (El Shaddai), and that He is an incomparable God (El Elyon)? As we associate with others, we become a reflection of those with whom we spend time (see Amos 3:3; Prov. 13:20). Can people in your life see that you have been hanging out with friends like those Daniel had?

I want to be like Daniel's friends.

Hananiah's, Mishael's, and Azariah's Babylonian captors changed their names but couldn't change their hearts. The three friends' hearts remained passionately committed to their incomparable God. I used to live in sin's Babylon. When Jesus delivered me from captivity, He changed not only my heart ("Therefore, if anyone is in Christ, he is a new creation..." [2 Cor. 5:17]), but He also changed my name ("...and will give him a white stone, and in the stone a new name written, which no man knoweth [except] he that receiveth it" [Rev. 2:17 KJV]).

I pray that you and I will be a reminder of God's gracious, incomparable help to those who know us—especially to those who are about to go into a fiery trial.

> *A despairing man should have the devotion of his friends...*
> (Job 6:14).

Reflection...

BREAD THAT ALWAYS RISES

Have you ever been given a jar of "starter" for sourdough bread? Well, I have been given a few and have followed the directions when I mixed up the bread dough, but seeing the bread rise to the top of the bowl has never been my experience. My friend Margo always has success with this "starter," and she always makes the most delicious bread. She has even given me some "starter" from her very own refrigerated jar, but the potion always dies in my refrigerator. Other women have declared that the "starter" worked for them, but I tend to be the exception to most circumstances. I did not give up trying to make this tasty sourdough bread until I had tried several times. With every attempt, I ended up with the most depressed looking loaves of bread; in fact, they looked more like cocoons for giant moths.

One day I was reading Deuteronomy 28 ("This woman can't make bread rise but she can understand the Book of Deuteronomy!"), and I came upon the blessings that God promised to His children who would fully obey the commands of the Lord. As I was reading the following list, I thought of a blessing that was missing from the list:

- blessed womb (verse 4)
- blessed basket and kneading trough (verse 5)
- blessed coming and going (verse 6)
- blessed barns (verse 8)
- blessed bank account (verse 12)
- always the top and never the bottom (verse 13)

As I read about blessed wombs, bubbling bread, bulging barns, and bursting bank accounts, I realized that—even though my sourdough bread remains at the "bottom of my kneading trough," my bank account has never been bursting, and I have sometimes felt as though I was at the bottom rather than the top—I am comforted by a blessing that is not in the above list: the blessing of an ever present Advocate who rises to defend me when I do not fully follow the Lord's commands (see 1 Jn. 2:1 KJV).

As the mystery of the sourdough bread cunningly escapes me, the greater mystery of a relationship with the Bread of Life has captured this baker's heart. This Bread of Life is always nourishing and comforting me, especially on those days when my kids ask, "Why are you baking giant moth cocoons?"

> *Your basket and your kneading trough will be blessed*
> (Deuteronomy 28:5).

REFLECTION...

____

____

____

____

____

____

____

____

____

____

____

____

JOY FOR A MOTHER'S INNERMOST BEING

While carrying our first child in my womb, I had so much anxiety about my lack of wisdom in the area of parenting. Because I came from such a painful home, I was so afraid that our home would contain the same chaos that I experienced as a child. I began to read everything I could about being a godly parent. I asked many questions of women whose children I knew and admired. I even asked children what they felt their parents did right. I must confess: I was desperate in my search. Parents whom I respected did one consistent thing: They took time to read to their children on a daily basis. This act of love requires some 15 to 20 minutes each day. As soon as our firstborn could sit up, I began reading daily to him. This was not only my privilege, but also that of my husband and any babysitter who would care for our children.

Thirteen years later, one night while Ken was out of town, Ben and I were having devotions together (Ben and his dad usually share this reading time together nightly). After we finished reading in the devotional book, Ben remarked about a verse that he had found in Matthew. I asked him, "When were you reading the Book of Matthew?" I assumed he would say in his Bible class at school.

To my surprise, Ben said, "Oh, I've been setting my alarm to wake me up 15 minutes earlier so I can read my Bible each day."

Of course my response was so intuitive, "Oh, really!!!"

Then I proceeded to share with Ben what Proverbs says about the joy that a wise son brings his father and mother. I shared with him how several times in the Book of Proverbs we are encouraged to keep the truth as close to us as a necklace around one's neck (see Prov. 3:3,22). When I prayed with Ben, my heart was full of praise for the work God is doing in Ben's private devotional world. I kissed Ben goodnight. Then, Ben walked toward the bathroom and said, "Mom, I love you, and I sure hope you like your new necklace." I confess: I was overwhelmed.

I have often run at a "full-throttle pace," but I can honestly say that I have never allowed busyness to rob our children of this special "soul-quieting time" with their mom or dad. If you've read the best-selling parenting book, *The Key to Your Child's Heart*, you will understand why this reading time was a Kendall family priority. Keeping a child's spirit open to the truth is the most awesome privilege and responsibility for any parent.

All those books, all those hours, all those moments will seem like a blink of an eye when the day comes that your children want to read and discover truth for themselves—when your time to read is over.

> *My son, if your heart is wise, then my heart will be glad; my inmost being will rejoice when your lips speak what is right* (Proverbs 23:15-16).

REFLECTION...

___

___

___

___

___

___

___

___

___

___

___

GOD'S LOVE LANGUAGE

On May 7, 1992, I finished reading my Bible and recorded the thought: "I delight God." It was such an awesome concept to consider the delight that I am capable of bringing to God. Psalm 16:3 defines the ones who delight God: "As for the saints who are in the land, they are the glorious ones in whom is *all my delight.*" Now, that is a verse I could "Selah" (pause and think about) for the rest of my days on planet Earth. When I think about delighting God and loving on Him, it is almost more than I can bear!

One year later, May 10, 1993, I journaled the following: "I have been thinking about Gary Chapman's teaching on the five love languages." As I thought about the different ways of showing love to others, suddenly I felt as though Jesus was sitting down right beside me on the couch. I heard Him say, "Jackie, what do you think My love language is?" At first, I was caught off guard by the question, and then I began to ponder it: *What fills God's love tank?*

You may think this question is ridiculous, but I really allowed myself to consider what God's love language is. I ran through Gary Chapman's list: touch, meaningful communication, acts of service, quality time, and gifts. I could see how all of them—except maybe touch—fill God's love tank.

Then the light went on in my heart, and I said to Jesus, "Your love language is faith/trust, isn't it?" The Lord reminded me of a scripture in Hebrews that validated my answer. The verse talks about the impossibility of ever totally satisfying the Lord without *faith.* Every challenging situation I face is an opportunity to love on the Lord. Every crisis I face that demands deep faith is a great time for loving on the Lord. As Philip Yancey says, "God doesn't want to be analyzed; He wants to be trusted." This is another way of saying, "He just wants to be loved by you."

David once wrote: "He brought me out into a spacious place; he rescued me because he delighted in me" (Ps. 18:19). David did not delight the Lord by being perfect; David delighted the Lord because he understood God's love language—trust and faith. Throughout the Psalms, you can find David trusting and loving on God during his darkest hours.

Here's a neat project: The next time you read the Psalms, whenever you see the word "trust", circle the word and let the circles be a reminder of God's love language.

The next time you face a trial, crisis, disappointment, broken dream, or heartbreak, remember that you are facing not only a chance to exercise your faith, but also an opportunity to "love on the Lord."

> *And without faith it is **impossible to please** God...*
> (Hebrews 11:6).

REFLECTION...

THE PERFECT FATHER'S DAY GIFT

Have you ever seen those ladders that have some "give" to them? They are sturdy but can bend a little when someone hurries up them. I told a group of women that I felt the perfect Father's Day gift would be this ladder. Some 80 women looked at me quite puzzled with this particular gift suggestion. I assured them that I had a perfectly good reason for such a gift. I reminded them about the study we had been doing on the topic, "When a Man Doesn't Need a Woman." We had been talking about a woman's tendency to want to control not only her children, but also her husband.

One of the most common techniques employed by women for control is *nagging*. Now, women hate the reference to nagging about as much as they hate the jokes about PMS. One day I mustered enough courage to read some of the common references on a nagging woman (see Prov. 19:13; 21:9,19; 27:15). One of the verses implies that a man is better off being a "roof-top dweller" (see Prov. 21:9) than living in a house with a nagging woman. As soon as I finished reading that verse, I saw a man placing a ladder on the side of his house and hurrying up the ladder to his roof. I started laughing at the thought of a man having to sit on his roof to escape his nagging wife and find a moment of peace with the God who made his wife!

Then I thought about the concept of a place that a man can hurry to when his wife begins to nag—so I brainstormed a trip to Home Depot where a woman could buy a ladder and place it on the side of her house with a ribbon around it for Father's Day. Then the next time Mommy starts nagging Daddy, he can calmly walk out the door, climb the ladder, and wait for her to calm down. I envisioned a whole neighborhood where men were sitting on their rooves just after dinner. Just think of all the fights that this ladder could prevent. What a quiet but potent visual reminder that nagging never changed one individual on planet Earth!

As I thought about the escape ladder, the Lord showed me that most men already have their escape routes down pat—whether it is tinkering in the garage, hunting every weekend (see Prov. 21:19), glaring at the TV, or even sitting behind the newspaper. Each man develops his own technique of muting his wife's voice. The saddest aspect of this reality is: When a man must develop a means of muting out his wife's nagging voice, he also carelessly mutes out her voice of love, encouragement, wisdom, and respect.

I was overwhelmed when I asked my husband how he felt when he heard my angry, nagging voice. He said, "I feel powerless." I now own that flexible ladder, and it is for me...I escape to a quiet place where my heavenly Bridegroom calms my heart so I nurture and not nag.

> *A quarrelsome wife is like a constant dripping on a rainy day; restraining her is like restraining the wind or grasping oil with the hand* (Proverbs 27:15-16).

Reflection...

____

____

____

____

____

____

____

____

____

____

The Longest Short Trip

My mom, brother Michael, sister Mary, and I went to Washington, D.C. for a 25-year Chrest family reunion. We got there a few days early so we could do some sightseeing. Then we decided to drive to Gaithersburg, MD, to surprise a group of relatives who had no idea that we had already arrived. We took off early in the morning; my brother was driving and I was the navigator. Thirty minutes into this one-hour trip, my mom said, "I think we are going the wrong way." We totally ignored her remarks because everyone knows that Mom needs directions to find her way out of her driveway. Mom kept insisting we were going the wrong way; we kept ignoring her remarks. Two hours later, we pulled over to ask directions, only to discover that we had driven for two hours in the direction opposite our destination. We were stunned, Mom was grinning, and Mary was laughing hysterically. Michael and I were completely frustrated by our own stubbornness and unwillingness to listen.

While reading the Book of Deuteronomy, I discovered a group of people who took "the longest short trip." Their prolonged trip made our journey look like a mere U-turn. It took Israel 40 years to reach the Promised Land. The actual traveling distance between Horeb and Kadesh Barnea takes 11 days. Mathematically, I cannot figure the ratio of 11 days to 14,600+ days, but I do know there is a big difference. What caused such a prolonged trip? What made this the longest short trip in history? No, I was *not* navigating for Moses and neither was my mom!

The journey for Israel was *prolonged* because of the people's *lack of faith.* Moses and the people roamed the desert for 40 years. Their lack of faith in the One navigating the trip was manifested by their murmuring and complaining in the presence of God's miraculous leadership. "In spite of this [all the miracles], you did not trust in the Lord your God" (Deut. 1:32). When Michael and I doubted Mom's word, we had grounds for our doubts. When Israel doubted God's Word through Moses, they had no grounds for their doubts. God mercifully let them roam for 40 years, like my mom let us drive for two hours the wrong way. He also provided for them the whole time they were roaming in the desert (see Deut. 2:7). His mercy also reminds me of the way my mother did not rub it in when our trip to Gaithersburg took five hours rather than one hour.

Often when the road gets rough, we are tempted to grumble, complain, and assume we are going the wrong way. Rough roads and barren deserts are all part of the journey with Jesus to a place of abundance (see Ps. 66:10-12). We prolong our time in the desert when we don't listen to the One trying to tell us the way we need to go (like good ol' Mom in the backseat that day). Jesus is taking us on a "potentially short trip to a place of abundance." It can take us 11 days or 40 years. Daily I am learning to listen to the Navigator. And next time, I am going to listen to Mom too!

> *These forty years the LORD your God has been with you, and **you have not lacked anything*** (Deuteronomy 2:7c).

Reflection...

____

____

____

____

____

____

____

____

____

A HEAVENLY HUG

Do you sometimes feel like you need a big hug? I heard a preacher talk about a big man walking up to him after a very moving message. Instead of asking the preacher to pray for him, the man said, "Can I have a hug?" Sometimes we need a hug, and in that moment there is no one we can turn to.

Years ago, as a single youth pastor, my husband was driving home after a long day of ministry to young people, and he realized how very lonely he felt. He loved working for Jesus, but that evening he was feeling particularly lonely. He began talking to the Lord about his loneliness when he suddenly felt a *presence* in his car. He felt a big hug that just warmed him from the top of his head to the tip of his toes. Now, Ken is not an emotional person, so this experience really caught him off guard and he felt as though he were experiencing a "meltdown." His heart was full of the presence of Jesus, and he was overwhelmed by a "heavenly hug."

Recently a young Christian mentioned going through a very difficult time: She felt as if she were in the "dead of winter" spiritually. Sylvia was driving in her car to visit someone in the hospital (which is very difficult for her) when she suddenly felt as though someone reached from behind the driver's seat and gave her a big hug. At first she was startled, then she was captivated by this comforting gesture from the Father. Both Ken and Sylvia felt this heavenly hug while driving in their cars, but I do not think God's comforting presence is only available in cars. I believe the Heavenly Hugger is available in hospital rooms, funeral homes, lonely hotel rooms, and during the darkest night or the brightest day.

I have met hundreds of people who know volumes about God but who only have pamphlets full of experiences with God. H. Blackaby, the author of *Experiencing God*, has said, "You will never be satisfied to just *know about God.*

Knowing God only comes through *experience* as He reveals Himself to you." I know that a person can experience God without ever feeling "hugged by God." But I also believe that we limit our experiences with God because we have Him in such a tight and confining box. Jesus is literally anxious to reveal more of Himself to His children. Are you sometimes skeptical about intimacy with God? I used to be...but the Spirit of "PaPa Sir" (see Gal. 4:6) who dwells within me has confronted my skepticism, and He has transformed my perception from *God* to *Father God*.

I have been hugged by Father God when I did not even know how needy I was. What a heritage for God's kids—our heavenly Father, the great "Heavenly Hugger."

> *...Let the beloved of the LORD rest secure in him, for he shields him all day long, and the one the LORD loves rests between his shoulders* (Deuteronomy 33:12).

REFLECTION...

____

HOW BOLDLY CAN WE PRAY?
KNOCKING AT MIDNIGHT

In Luke chapter 11 Jesus teaches His disciples how to pray. While rereading this familiar passage, I almost missed a most precious nugget: Luke 11:5-8. In these verses Jesus tells a story of a *very inconvenient request from a friend at midnight.* The friend grants the request *not because of friendship,* but because of the *petitioner's persistence,* e.g. *boldness.*

I decided to look up *persistence/boldness.* Hold onto your hats! The Greek word *anaiden,* for persistence/boldness, means "unabashed audacity," "shameless boldness," "brazen persistence displayed," "in the pursuit of something," "an insistence characterized by rudeness."

Wow, when was the last time you or I prayed with "unabashed audacity" and "shameless boldness"? As I pondered this question, the Lord reminded me of the prayer life of my first mentor. As Mamie Hinch prayed with such "shameless boldness," I would wonder if my confidence in God would ever be strong enough for me to pray with such glorious audacity.

I cry out to God without holding back... (Ps. 77:1 NLT).

As I thought about this boldness in prayer, the Lord reminded me of Heb. 4:16. This speaks about coming before the throne of God with confidence. The Greek word for confidence, *parresia,* means "freedom in speaking all that one thinks," "confident boldness in speaking," "plainness and exactness of speech."

I am fired up that Jesus reminds me today that "shameless boldness" is a critical aspect of prevailing prayer power. May we pray with holy audacity and shameless boldness, because prayer can do whatever God can do.

So let us come boldly to the throne of our gracious God. There we will receive His mercy, and we will find grace to help us when we need it (Hebrews 4:16 NLT).

REFLECTION...

A NO-EXCUSE WOMAN

Have you ever been distracted by daily demands? Have you ever felt crippled by your circumstances? Have you ever gone to bed exhausted emotionally? I discovered a woman in the Word of God who did not let her daily demands, crippling circumstances, and emotional exhaustion keep her from doing what was right in a major crisis. No, it is not the superwoman described in Proverbs 31, but she was a relative of the author of the Book of Proverbs.

I found this "no-excuse woman" in First Samuel 25—you guessed it: Abigail. She is described as an intelligent, beautiful woman. It is obvious that this woman of understanding had no choice regarding a mate, because her husband, Nabal, is described as a churlish man, which in our modern language means: "a real jerk." Abigail had no choice concerning her marriage partner, but she did have a choice in how she would live while married to such a mean and unapproachable man (see 1 Sam. 25:3,17).

Abigail did not use the excuse of being married to a wicked man to keep her from making a critical, wise choice in a life-threatening matter. Her servants came to her with the crisis situation because they knew that you "do not present a reasonable request to an unreasonable person (Nabal)." When she was told of the approaching disaster, Abigail quickly did what was right (see 1 Sam. 25:18). Even though she could have been emotionally crippled by the life-threatening circumstances, she wisely moved into an action that kept David and 400 soldiers from killing all the men in her household.

Abigail lived with a cruel man, which is an emotional drain. I believe that the God of Israel must have shown her how to use good judgment rather than excuses when faced with hard decisions and draining demands. She did not use her husband's evil dealings as an excuse to hold weekly "pity parties."

Abigail was not codependent toward Nabal because she saw him for what he was. "May my lord pay no attention to that wicked man Nabal. He is just like his name—his name is Fool, and folly goes with him" (1 Sam. 25:25a). She made no excuses for Nabal's harsh response when David and his men needed a blessing.

An anointed earthly king blessed Abigail for her good judgment, and her heavenly King sustained her while she was married to a fool. When the fool died, the earthly king took her as his bride (see 1 Sam. 25:40). Of course, the moral of this story is not: Do the right thing and God will kill your foolish husband and give you a king in his place. The moral of this story is: If Abigail can bless an earthly king while married to a fool, we can bless our heavenly King, regardless of the biographical sketch of our mate.

> *May you be blessed for your good judgment and for keeping me from bloodshed...* (1 Samuel 25:33).

REFLECTION...

____

____

____

____

____

____

____

____

____

____

____

____

A MISSIONARY TO BEVERLY HILLS

Now, the title above may seem to contain a contradiction of terms: missionary and Beverly Hills. In LeeAnn's case, these terms are completely compatible. A missionary is one who is sent to a foreign place to bring the good news of Jesus to those who have not heard. Trust me, Beverly Hills would be a foreign place for many of us. Almost on a weekly basis, LeeAnn encounters another person who does not know God's way to heaven. Oh, they have heard mumblings about mystical mountain-climbing efforts to heaven, but very few know the revealed truth of God.

When LeeAnn first told me that her husband's promotion would transport them from Orlando to Beverly Hills, I immediately thought of the famous people that LeeAnn would rub shoulders with, and I just grinned—because I knew that LeeAnn would never allow celebrity or star status to keep her from looking for every little niche that she could possibly squeeze the truth about Jesus into.

She found a church and told the leadership of her willingness to host a Bible study in her home. When the sign-up sheets were sent out, no one signed up for her group. She called me, and I told her God would show her the women that He had in mind for a "90210 Bible study." It has been so exciting to hear about the women who have found themselves at this Bible study.

After telling a rich young man what he must do to inherit eternal life (see Mk. 10:17-22), Jesus turned to His disciples and said, "How hard it is for the rich to enter the kingdom of God" (Mk. 10:23). It has been so fabulous to see God use LeeAnn to scale the walls of difficulty in the lives of the rich and famous—and boldly tell them about her Jesus. It is so hard for the rich to ever believe that there isn't enough money, fame, or things in the world to satisfy their hungry hearts. I am so grateful that God placed LeeAnn right in the hub of this mentality and gave her the courage to challenge this vanity.

LeeAnn could waste so many hours by being self-consumed as many of her rich and famous neighbors do. Her passion for God keeps her from squandering the gift of time that she has been given. She is a witness, whether she is shopping at Bloomingdale's or playing on a playground with her daughter and the other children who are there with their nannies. Her Christianity has permeated her role as a wife and mother. She shines in a crowd because her inward beauty magnifies her outward beauty. She is not only a missionary in Beverly Hills, but she also supports missions and goes regularly on mission trips. You should have seen her on a rough job site on a mission trip to Quito, Ecuador. She was a champion girl scout from Beverly Hills.

> *Brothers, think of what you were when you were called. Not many of you were wise...influential...of noble birth* (1 Corinthians 1:26).

REFLECTION...

____

____

____

____

____

____

____

____

____

____

____

A PRICELESS BELT IN A TRASH CAN

For more than 14 years, my mother has strung pearls for stores on prestigious Worth Avenue of Palm Beach, Florida. One day while delivering some work to one of these stores, she was in the back of the store when she noticed a beautiful belt lying in a trash can. When she asked about the belt, the owner remarked that she had "no use" for the belt any longer. My mother, being the humble woman that she is, asked if she could give the throwaway belt to her daughter. The owner agreed, and Mom took the beautiful belt out of the trash can.

My mom looked at the belt to see why it was "useless." Were some of the beads torn off the leather, or was the buckle broken? After examining the belt more closely, my mom realized that the belt was not only in perfect condition, but was also worth at least $300. The detailed beadwork mounted on leather was awesome! My mom couldn't wait to give the beautiful belt to her oldest child. I never wear the belt without remembering where it was taken from—a trash can in a Palm Beach store.

While reading in Jeremiah 13, I came across another "priceless belt in a trash can." This belt was not created by artists in China; this belt was a people that God had chosen for His glory. What had rendered the belt "useless"? The buckle was not broken, and the beadwork was not torn from the leather. This belt (this people) was useless because of stubborn hearts and a refusal to listen to God's Word.

These people had been chosen and pulled close to God, as close as one wraps a belt around one's waist. The privilege of closeness and intimacy with Almighty God should have resulted in a people who brought God praise and honor, people chosen to be wrapped around God as a priceless belt or a trusted confidant. "The Lord confides in those who fear Him; He makes His covenant known to them" (Ps. 25:14). Being one of God's daughters, I do not want to be found "useless" because of my own stubbornness or be found in a "trash can" because I would not listen to the Father. I find security in being wrapped around the Father and of being of priceless value to Him as He confides in me (see Jn. 14:21; Eph. 1:9).

> *"These wicked people, who refuse to listen to my words, who follow the stubbornness of their hearts...will be like this belt—completely useless! For as a belt is bound around a man's waist, so I bound the whole house of Israel and the whole house of Judah to me," declares the Lord, "to be my people for my renown and praise and honor..."* (Jeremiah 13:10-11).

Reflection...

____

____

____

____

____

____

____

____

____

____

____

____

____

____

HOW DO YOU SAY GOOD-BYE TO SHAME?

Although we know that Jesus died to pay for our sins, some Christians are constantly assaulted by satan's favorite tool—shame. Although forgiven believers know that there is no *condemnation* in Christ (see Rom. 8:1), we still seem to struggle with shame. Why does shame keep such a tenacious hold on so many Christians? Last night in church, the worship leader read a passage of scripture, and the Lord so rocked my world that I wanted to jump out of my seat, run to the platform, grab a microphone, and share what God showed me. Wisdom kept me seated, so I share this with you.

The passage was Luke 7:36-50. In my Bible it has a subtitle: "Jesus Anointed by a Sinful Woman." I know this scripture well and used it in the first chapter of my book *Lady in Waiting*—describing a woman's reckless abandon to Jesus. As I looked more closely at the passage, something new came into focus. This sinful, notorious woman walked into a most condemning situation: the home of Simon the Pharisee. It would be like a prostitute showing up for a covered dish dinner at the pastor's house! This sinful woman did not allow condemning shame to keep her from anointing and kissing the feet of the Holy One of Israel. Now, how did a *sinful* woman walk past a judgmental, self-righteous man like Simon? This sinner was so focused on Jesus Christ that she was not tripped up by a "shaming Simon"!! This person did something so radical—so passionate. Her single-minded attention on Jesus kept her from being frozen in her steps by *shame's chilly finger of condemnation.*

The judgmental "shaming Simons" of this world are daily used by satan (see Rev.12: 10-11) to accuse, confuse and trip up God's less-than-perfect children. When a believer focuses on Jesus, the "shaming Simons" of this world wield no power over that believer. However, when struggling believers focus on a Simon's comments, they are stopped in their tracks and they never reach the feet of Jesus. We are to come *boldly* unto the throne of grace (see Heb. 4:15-16). We must resist the "shaming Simons" who continually whisper how "unworthy" we are.

Focus on the forgiving Savior rather than the judgmental Simons.

Do you know how God views our failures?

- He expects them.
- He forgives them.
- He uses them.

The following memory verses will break the finger of any "shaming Simon":

> *Do not be afraid; you will not suffer shame. Do not fear disgrace; you will not be humiliated. You will forget the shame of your youth…* (Isaiah 54:4).

> *Instead of their shame my people will receive a double portion, and instead of disgrace they will rejoice in their inheritance; and so they will inherit a double portion in their land, and everlasting joy will be theirs.* (Isaiah 61:7).

Whenever you get ready to worship Jesus, don't be surprised if "shaming Simon" is in the room—and when this happens, focus on Jesus. Boldly kiss His feet and ignore the groan of a "shaming Simon" in the background!

> *…and the one who trusts in Him will never be put to shame* (Romans 9:33).

Reflection…

____

____

SURRENDER YOUR JUNIOR GOD BADGE AT THE DOOR, PLEASE

Where did this "Junior God badge" originate? Who was the first person who struggled with the desire to run the universe, or at least his or her part of the planet? I don't mean to pick on our dear mother, Eve, but she was the first woman who decided that control was better than dependence on God. Now, she was not the first "being" that wanted the Junior God title—that belongs to lucifer, whose "love song" of independence (see Isa. 14:12-15) transported him from heaven to hell. Now he roams planet Earth in an attempt to enlist people in his choir!

This Junior God badge mentality manifests itself in the basic need to control. The woman with this propensity will actually feel the responsibility of living out the very characteristics of God. I know this woman very well, and I have experienced all her propensities.

For example, the omnipresent woman can be found zooming through the day, rushing here and there to be everything to everybody. She is doing her best to be everywhere for everyone so that she can keep everyone in her world happy. This omnipresent woman ends up frustrated and fatigued.

The omnipotent woman has unrealistic, grandiose expectations of herself. Common phrases used by her throughout the day are: "I can do it…I'll get it…I'll fix it…I'll do it…." She is so driven to make everyone happy that she even worries about God's needs.

The omniscient woman is driven by the need to be all-knowing (constantly reading, attending seminars, etc) so she can use her knowledge to control, pressure, and manipulate those in her world. Controlling them for their good is her reason—but also her blindspot.

The sovereign woman manifests the heart of the need to control. "I am in charge so no one will get hurt." She is afraid to surrender the terrible burden she is carrying—the burden of always wanting life on her terms.

Only God Almighty can be all-knowing, all-powerful, and always present—never fatigued, frustrated, drained, aggravated, and burned out. Wow, I am already tired and it is only 2:07 p.m.! I think I am going to remove my Junior God badge and put it back in the junk drawer in my kitchen. The Lord has given me the freedom to wear the badge—if I want to burn out myself and others. Once again, I choose to remove my Junior God badge, pour myself a Diet Coke, and let God be in charge; I am just too tired.

> *For anyone who enters God's rest also rests from his own work, just as God did from his* (Hebrews 4:10).

Reflection...

LIBERATING THE CONTROL FREAK
GOD: THE ULTIMATE AGENT OF CAUSATION

Recently the Lord gave my daughter something in her devotions that has captured my attention. I can't escape the impact. Jessica was studying John 17 when she came upon verse 17: "Sanctify them by the truth; your word is truth." Jessica studied the Greek words for "sanctify" and found a definition that thrilled her: "God is the ultimate agent of causation."

That phrase is so incredible when you allow yourself to remove your "Junior God badge" and ponder the depth of what you see in people every day.

Causation is defined in Webster's as "the process of causing." To cause is defined as "to effect by command, authority, or force."

For the woman who longs to be completely delivered from her Evette-like (Eve-like) addiction to control, this definition is *most liberating.* The sanctification of a life is the result of Jehovah-mekoddishkem's (the Lord who sanctifies you) glorious "causation" in a person's heart. This reality has changed what I pray for people. Now I pray that God will sanctify them "through and through" and then I can release the outcome of my longings because I know who the agent of causation is—*not me, but God.*

Six years ago, a single gal named Jodi exhorted me with the phrase "It is not about you, but God." That young woman understood that God is the ultimate agent of causation. He alone changes the human heart.

If you love someone whose heart needs changing, just keep asking Jehovah-mekoddishkem to sanctify them through and through.

I can return to the Lord's daily assignments with joy and confidence in the ultimate agent of causation—El Elyon the Most High God.

P.S. Sometimes as spouses we want to be the ultimate agent of causation…

Sometimes as parents we want to be the ultimate agent of causation…

Sometimes as friends we want to be the ultimate agent of causation…

Sometimes as ministry leaders we want to be the ultimate agent of causation.

P.S.S. Again…I remove my Junior God badge. I have pierced too many holes in my clothes by continually re-attaching it.

I will give you a new heart…And I will put my Spirit in you and move you to follow my decrees and be careful to keep my laws (Ezekial 36: 26,27).

Reflection…

FRUITFUL IN SUFFERING

After speaking at a youth camp in North Carolina, Ken and I and our children decided to drive home that evening so we could sleep in our own beds. We arrived home at about 2:00 a.m. and put our sleeping children in bed. Since we noticed a large number of messages on our answering machine, we began listening to them as we prepared to go to bed.

The first voice was the shouting of my youngest brother: "Jackie, call us at JFK emergency room!" The next message was the calm voice of my sister-in-law, pleading: "Jackie, please call us right away." The next message was Ken's mother, saying, "Where are you, children? Call home now!" The fourth call was a dear Christian friend, who said: "We are so sorry about your sister; call us if there is anything we can do."

I said to Ken, "Which sister (I had four)? What is going on?" Ken insisted on calling his mom first, and then I planned to call my mom.

When I heard Ken say, "Oh no," I began to cry. I did not know what had happened, but I knew something horrible had taken place. While Ken and I had been speaking Friday night to young people about saying "no" to drugs, alcohol, and premarital sex, my sister, Bobbie, was dying at the JFK emergency room from a drug overdose.

The news of her suicide was the most painful thing I had ever experienced. I felt as though I had entered an emotional coma. I knew that Jesus wanted to comfort and sustain me, but the grief inside screamed so loud that—for a brief moment—His voice was drowned out. Because He is a man of sorrows who is acquainted with grief, He very patiently waited for me to throw myself into His comforting arms.

One year later (early morn on Mother's Day) in the same emergency room, my dad died of sudden heart failure. He was not ready for eternity, and that reality had me in a state of grief far deeper than words could ever express. I had been trying to reach my father spiritually for 24 years. As my brother drove me home from the emergency room, I kept thinking about facing our children, who had been praying for years for Grandpa's salvation. All I knew to do was weep with them, hold them, and rely on the only One who could comfort us in this unbearable circumstance. When I went to bed that night, I told Jesus that I did not know how He could possibly comfort me in the face of such a horrifying reality.

The next morning, Jesus gave a word to a dear friend (Margo) who called and asked me to look at the name of Joseph's second born. When I read the name *Ephraim* my heart jumped within me and peace began to flood my soul. Jesus said, "Jackie, I am going to plant a garden in the center of your pain, a garden that will bless not only your life but also the lives of many others." Out of my sister's suicide and my dad's hopeless death something beautiful has come. I now wear a gold bracelet with the name *Ephraim* as a daily reminder that pain is an opportunity for the planting of another garden. (Note: In 1994, another of my siblings committed suicide. By the grace of God, I continue to learn about being fruitful in suffering.)

> *The second son he named Ephraim and said, "It is because God has made me fruitful in the land of my suffering"* (Genesis 41:52).

REFLECTION...

____

____

____

____

____

A BROKEN DREAM IN THE MAKING

I am a planner, a dreamer, and a list maker—I get as much fun from planning and anticipating an event as from the actual event! But the downside of this grand adventure comes when the event never materializes after all my dreaming and planning. When I was a young Christian, I would always preface my dreams and plans with the biblical expression, "If the Lord wills...." Using that phrase in front of my plans always reminded me that I needed to yield my plans, as well as my hopes and dreams, to God. "Commit to the Lord whatever you do, and your plans will succeed" (Prov. 16:3).

A couple of years into my Christian walk, after hearing me use the phrase, "If the Lord wills," an older Christian said, "You do not need to use that phrase to try to sound spiritual." Now, I never thought of the phrase as a way of sounding spiritual. I used that phrase to remind myself who is ultimately in charge of my life's blueprints. Fearing others would think that I was using a "Christianese" expression, I stopped saying, "If the Lord wills" or "Lord willing."

When I grew older and (thank God) wiser, I realized that the phrase, "Lord willing," is not only a wonderful reminder for the one who uses these two words, but also for the one who hears them. This generation is so afraid of spiritualizing and over-using Christian lingo that we have forgotten the awesome reality that God's Word is supernaturally empowered (see Heb. 4:12). Whether it's a verse or an expression used in God's Word, we need to be careful not to discard it like some type of colloquial slang.

Why did the Holy Spirit tell us to preface our blueprints and dreams with the expression, "If the Lord wills"? I think one of the reasons is to remind us to give our blueprints and dreams to the Lord for His authorization on a continual basis. I am only 30 years old in Jesus, but one thing I know for sure:

"Every expectation,
every plan,
every dream
not yielded to God,
is a potential broken dream in the making."

I am still a planner, dreamer, and list maker but I am using the phrase "If the Lord wills" more than ever these days.

> *Now listen, you who say, "Today or tomorrow we will go to this or that city, spend a year there, carry on business and make money" ... Instead, you ought to say, "If it is the LORD's will, we will live and do this or that." As it is, you boast and brag. All such boasting is evil* (James 4:13,15-16).

REFLECTION...

SPEECHLESS IN THE PRESENCE OF PAIN

Sitting in a restaurant across from a beautiful single woman, I listened to her personal story of pain. She had been married for a few years and had been trying to conceive a child. In the meantime, her best friend (who was single) told her that she was pregnant. What irony! Her unmarried friend was with child while she continued childless. The irony turned into trauma when her single friend told her who the father was—her husband. Can you comprehend the devastation caused in this beautiful woman's heart? She had been betrayed not only by her husband, but also by her best friend. Have you experienced a similarly crushing emotional blow?

She told how she had put her life on hold emotionally after her husband divorced her. Such a response is totally understandable. When she had finished her story, I was speechless (which is not my normal state of being). I sat stunned, praying for several minutes. Then the Lord graciously nudged me and said, "Jackie, I am not intimidated by trauma. In fact, I can be closer than ever during such painful times." After this heavenly nudge, I took a chance and I challenged her to give her broken heart, her empty arms, and her loneliness to Jesus. By faith, I assured her that Jesus could touch and heal the ragged tear in her heart.

She accepted the challenge, and Jesus not only performed major surgery on her heart, but He also taught her how to resist feeling sorry for herself and stop living in the arena of bitterness. After she made the choice of recklessly abandoning herself to Jesus as Lord, she was free to serve Him. Jesus transformed her from a crushed, brokenhearted single woman into a fearless witness for Jesus. Years later, a godly man fell in love with this single woman who had been using her free time to serve the Head Surgeon who repaired her broken heart.

When someone tells me about deep personal pain, my initial response is often speechlessness. In those moments of stunned silence, the Holy Spirit reminds me that the "God of *all* comfort" is ready and available. Sometimes a person is not ready to turn to God for comfort. It is very tempting to usurp God's role and try to be *the* comforter. The problem with being this empathetic comforter is the brevity of the effect of our comfort. Only comfort from God lasts into the late hours of the night and throughout the many lonely days ahead. I carefully listen to their pain (even crying when they cry), but I persistently point toward the only One who can truly heal a broken heart. David wrote about the nearness of God when the pain was the deepest. He knew firsthand that only God gives lasting hope and comfort.

> *The LORD is close to the brokenhearted and saves those who are crushed in spirit* (Psalm 34:18).

Reflection...

Ginger's Song of Victory

After a very loud, upbeat concert with the group New Song, our pastor said that someone very special was going to give a testimony. Onto the platform walked a petite blonde. She began to tell us that the Lord had asked her to stand before the congregation and give Him glory and praise. Now that would not seem like a hard assignment from the Lord, unless you understand the context of Ginger's life.

In only eight years of marriage, Ginger and Kevin had faced many trials—the deaths of their two sons, then a miscarriage, and questions as to whether Ginger could bear more children. Ginger never allowed her childlessness to keep her from being a blessing to someone else's children as an elementary school teacher. Ginger came to accept childlessness as her cross to bear. The cross became heavier when Christmas came, and with this happy time of year she also received word that her precious father had fast-moving, incurable cancer. The questions came as quickly as the cancer came. *How does someone so full of life, strength, and youth get a disease that will take all his strength away so quickly? Haven't I suffered enough with the deaths of two sons and the unfulfilled desire to have children? Why, God, why me?*

While her dad was dying, Ginger was diagnosed with cancer. As Ginger battled for life against this invading virus, a bigger battle was raging within—this battle was the strong challenge to her faith. The challenge came in the form of a painful "why, God?" The battle raged stronger—her dad was dying back home in Alabama while she was waging war on her own cancer in the hospital in West Palm Beach.

Ginger went before our congregation (1,000 people) that night to publicly declare who had won the battle against the painful "why, God?" Only God's grace enables anyone to win against the infamous "why, God?" Ginger has won against so many challenges to her faith, and I can hear her battle song of victory:

I will declare God's goodness in the face of death,
I will declare God's goodness in the face of loss,
I will declare God's goodness in the face of my own cancer,
I will declare God's goodness in the face of broken dreams.

She concluded her testimony with a powerful statement of faith: "I have learned to trust Him, even when I don't understand" (see Isa. 40:28). Her willingness to live without understanding is the manifestation of her deep faith. I know she is a candidate for God's hall of fame, whose inductees are nominated because of their faith. Living without all the answers is the very heart of the life of faith. (Ginger's cancer went into remission, and she and Kevin adopted a precious baby girl. Six years later Ginger won the ultimate victory over cancer...heaven.)

> *As you do not know the path of the wind, or how the body is formed in a mother's womb, so you cannot understand the work of God, the Maker of all things* (Ecclesiastes 11:5).

Reflection...

A MIRACLE WORKER

The movie *The Miracle Worker* left such a lasting impression on me through watching a human being with a Herculean task daily attempt the impossible. On January 3, 1992, I watched another "miracle worker." This time the star was not Anne Sullivan but my husband, Ken Kendall. I watched Ken preach his younger brother Mark's funeral. The church was packed to the wall. More than half the audience were not believers (mostly business associates of the Kendall Companies). The Lord showed Ken that he was going to do the impossible: Ken would use Mark's expressions and gestures to preach the gospel through Mark, titled "A Message From Heaven."

Ten years earlier Ken had performed Mark's wedding, and then the Lord led him to preach at his funeral. As I listened to Ken, I whispered to both our children, "You are watching a miracle. This is not possible to do in one's own strength." As I watched Ken share such a powerful challenge, I knew I was a "miracle watcher." The Lord not only gave Ken the message but also the method of sharing the truth that would challenge and comfort in the midst of grief.

Later that day, I watched another miracle as Ken shared with Tony (a family friend) the good news of knowing the God of all comfort personally. I was again a "miracle watcher" as I witnessed Ken leading Tony in a prayer to receive Jesus Christ.

Eighteen months prior to this funeral, I had spoken at the funeral of my younger sister, who had committed suicide. I knew the task was impossible, but I also knew that "impossible" simply means "possible with God." One year later, I was making arrangements for my father's funeral; six months later Ken was doing his brother's funeral. Three immediate family members died within 18 months, and our friends were "miracle watchers," as they saw God sustain us.

At each funeral, the *God of all comfort* hugged us on the inside while others hugged us on the outside: These were holy moments. Being sustained by God through three seasons of grief (back to back) proved to our family, without a doubt, that God's grace is sufficient. Every trial, every heartbreak, every tragic loss is a chance for another episode of *The Miracle Worker*, God.

> *As a mother comforts her child, so will I comfort you... When you see this, your heart will rejoice and you will flourish like grass; the hand of the LORD will be made known to his servants...* (Isaiah 66:13-14).

REFLECTION...

____

____

____

____

____

____

____

____

____

____

____

____

____

____

____

____

GIFT FOR THE GRIEVING

Before March 23, 1990, I always felt inadequate whenever I was told about death visiting a family I knew. Whether I was going to the funeral, viewing, service, or the following wake, I felt speechless and ill-prepared to comfort those in mourning. Once, after a funeral and wake, Ken asked me, "Why do we have a viewing, a funeral service, and a get-together afterwards?"

I said, "I really don't know." The whole grief process was really a mystery to both Ken and me.

Then grief came knocking loudly at our door with the suicide of my younger sister, Bobbie. Grief continued to bang on our door with the sudden death of my father, and grief almost punched a hole in our door with the shocking death of Ken's younger brother. With each death came more understanding about the grief process and the "gift for the grieving."

This gift can be given by anyone who loves the people who have lost a loved one. It involves time, attention, patience, listening—and no rushing of the grief process. Too often, well-meaning (but blind) Christians try to hurry a person through the grief process. They preach at the one in mourning, rather than listen and pray. In their preaching, they encourage the grieving person to shove living feelings underground—only to be resurrected at a later date in an even more grievous way. Being robbed of the freedom to grieve is often as potent as death.

This "gift for the grieving" was given to Jacob's sons by Pharaoh (see Gen. 50:1-14) when their father, Jacob, died. Pharaoh ordered the people to mourn for him 70 days (10 weeks for a stranger). The funeral procession contained not only family but also all the dignitaries of Egypt. When they reached the burial place, they wept *loudly and bitterly*. The healing that takes place during a loud lamenting is only understood by those who have been given the freedom to weep deeply. Too often Christians are constrained to a silent stream of tears...no loud weeping. We have too often been robbed of the "gift for the grieving" by preconceived ideas about proper grieving for the believer. If you postpone grieving, the grief does not go away...you only increase the debt owed to grief and actually *prolong the grieving process.*

A counselor once asked a counselee, "Did you cry when your brother was murdered?"

The counselee responded, "Why cry? It wouldn't bring him back."

The counselor wisely replied, "You're right. But it would have brought you back." Whatever powerful emotions (grief, rejection, shame, anger, hate, etc.) we bury, we also bury a part of ourselves. When faced with those who mourn, encourage them to grieve—to keep them alive and not bury them, too. Grief is so deep, but not deeper than God's comfort.

Mourn with those who mourn (Romans 12:15b).

Reflection...

A MAN TOUCHED DEEPLY BY MY PAIN

One night we had some friends over for dinner. As the children ate quickly and went into the garage to play, the conversation at the dinner table moved to an emotionally charged topic. The wife (guest) began to share her heart openly, which resulted in her beginning to weep. Ken and I both looked at her husband—we expected him to move over close to her and put a comforting arm around her. We watched as her husband sat totally still and appeared detached emotionally from her. Finally, I jumped up and put my arm around her. She continued to cry and even remarked about her husband's emotional detachment during her display of painful feelings.

So much is happening in America in relation to the healing of the masculine soul. This focus on the masculine soul has even captured and challenged the attention of the Body of Christ. Organizations are being formed where men are being encouraged to "become emotionally reattached." More and more men are looking for mentors and accountability groups.

So ironic to me is the concept that a man who is capable of "feeling someone else's pain" is considered very exceptional, as though women are the only ones really capable of such compassion and sympathy. I have experienced several "lively" discussions recently where men have complained that "women are trying to make men into women in this area of feelings." I understand their concern, but I believe that men have been shut down by a generational cycle of selfish detachment from feelings—a cycle that also shuts down compassion and sympathy.

Every woman's dream is a man who is not frustrated when she weeps. Every woman's fantasy is a man who can sympathize with the things that hurt her—a man who comforts her, rather than preaches at her when she is weeping. Well, I have found the perfect man of my dreams in Jesus Christ, and as my husband becomes more like Jesus, he, too, is becoming the man of my dreams.

Jesus, all God and all man, was totally in touch with his feelings. He was capable of not only sympathy but also compassion. Jesus is described in Hebrews as a high priest who can be touched by our pain. The Greek word for "touched" actually means "be touched with a feeling of…." So, Jesus, a man's man, was comfortable with all types of feelings and human frailty. Being detached from emotions and incapable of weeping with those who weep is not Christlikeness. Being uncomfortable in the presence of weakness, lacking compassion for those who struggle, is not spiritual maturity. The more a man can sympathize, the more he reflects the compassion that was in Jesus' eyes.

> *For we do not have a high priest who is unable to sympathize with our weaknesses* (Hebrews 4:15a).

REFLECTION…

____

____

____

____

____

____

____

____

____

____

____

____

Regina's Story

I was teaching a seminar for single women on "Waiting for God's Best" (now in book form as *Lady in Waiting*). One young lady held my attention throughout the time I taught—her beaming countenance was like a magnet for me. Afterwards, she stood in line to speak to me, and when she introduced herself, I remarked about her gorgeous red hair and wonderful smile. She was so excited because she was coming to the town where I live to attend a local Christian college. She would be an education major, as I had been, and her zeal for the Lord reminded me of myself in college.

I saw her only a couple of times in West Palm Beach, and she always had that glow about her. I meet so many people, and I am horrible about remembering names, but Regina's name I never forgot: the redhead on fire for Jesus.

One Easter Sunday afternoon, as my brother-in-law was showing us his school annual, he became especially anxious to show us the dedication pages where the college had given a special tribute to a dear friend of our family. As he opened to the memorial page honoring Dr. Billie, across the page from her picture was a wonderful picture of Regina. I gasped in shock because the students were memorializing the death of such a soul winner—Regina. I asked Tim, "How did Regina die?"

His reply was too horrible to believe. Regina had gone bike riding. When she did not return, the search began. They found her body the next day—she had been raped and her throat had been slit. I was so shocked that I became quite hysterical for a moment. I wept for such a tragic death of a precious redhead living for Jesus. I had to calm down because the whole family wanted to know why I was weeping so hard. They did not know that I had been blessed in meeting Regina.

As I cried off and on for three days, I kept thinking about her parents aching for their loss. On the third day, my mourning moved into deep anger that godly parents raised a daughter for God's glory but that her destiny had become rape and murder. Of course, I was also selfishly thinking about such a horrible thing ever happening to our daughter, and the angry tears just kept flowing. Then the God of all comfort turned my anger into understanding through the Book of Job. The Lord showed me that He is capable of caring for us when we face our greatest loss. He assured me that His grace can travel as deep as a Grand Canyon of grief. He also showed me that Regina's parents will be given a glimpse of Him, like Job received. A glimpse will not answer all their questions, but it will give strength and hope to keep them from becoming spiritually barren. I have heard through others that God is using her parents, who are truly fruitful and not barren.

One glimpse of Him and hope begins to heal the heart's agony....

> *My ears had heard of you but now my eyes have seen you*
> (Job 42:5).

REFLECTION...

___

___

___

___

___

___

___

___

___

___

BLOSSOMS AFTER THE STORM

When we moved into our second home, one of my first concerns was the huge amount of tropical plants surrounding it. The house had won the landscaping award in a parade of homes contest. I knew that such beautiful plants do not grow without some attention and care. I was anxious because, instead of having a "green thumb," mine is black. I have single-handedly killed every living plant that I have ever been given. I took my "black thumb" to a nursery to find out the perfect fertilizer for the beautiful bird-of-paradise plants that line our entryway and the even more gorgeous white bird-of-paradise plants that grow outside the master-bath windows. The man told me what fertilizer I needed and when to apply the food to the plants. I went home feeling as though my "black thumb" had hope.

I began spreading the fertilizer and, in my enthusiasm, I put too much fertilizer on all the birds. I ended up "burning the buds" right in their stalks. I was so upset that I actually cried. These tropical plants were so special to me because they represented the first flower my son ever gave me. When Ben was only three years old, he told his dad that he had to get his mom a flower. Ken took Ben to a flower shop, and the first flower that caught Ben's eye was a beautiful bird-of-paradise.

Day after day, I had to walk past the buds burned in their stalks, and my heart just ached for the beauty that was burned by my "black thumb". How ironic to think I wanted to help the plants grow and my heavy-handed touch resulted in stunted growth! The fertilizer actually acted as a soil inhibitor. So often, good seed is kept from sprouting because of soil inhibitors. Similarly, in the lives of many people, the precious Word of God is kept from sprouting because of the soil inhibitors that are in the human heart.

Two months later, we had a tropical storm, and it rained for many hours. A few days after the storm, our daughter began to shout from the front porch. I arrived to see her pointing at a new bud. The rain had washed away the excess fertilizer, and the plant was now free to blossom. I became so excited that I jumped up and down on our porch. I started thinking about the storms of life and how they wash away the things that inhibit our growth. I have begun praying that God will send storms into the lives of people in whom I have planted the precious seed of truth. I have prayed for storms of freedom—freedom to blossom.

If you know someone in whom people have planted the "good seed" of God's Word, start praying for the soil-cleansing storm that will allow the sprouting and blossoming of the incorruptible seed.

> *Being born again, not of corruptible seed, but of incorruptible, by the word of God, which liveth and abideth for ever* (1 Peter 1:23 KJV).

Reflection...

___

___

___

___

___

___

___

___

___

___

___

THE GOVERNOR ON MY GAS PEDAL

One day while Rita was foil-frosting my hair in her kitchen, I was complaining about people who always want to slow me down. I told her how frustrated I get when certain individuals step in front of me just when I am ready to sprint forward. Rita said, "Oh, they are God-sent governors for your gas pedal."

I said, "What in the world is a governor for a gas pedal?" Well, I looked it up in a dictionary, which said: "a feedback device on a car or machine used to provide automatic control of speed, pressure and temperature."

So these people whom I find irritating are sometimes God-sent devices to control the speed of my daily life. Wow! I began to wonder if I could validate such a concept scripturally. Maybe you are already thinking of some "God-placed governors" in your life. I decided to look into the lives of three Bible characters.

First, I looked at King David. Immediately I realized that Saul was not only sandpaper for David's life, but also a God-sent governor. I realized that so many of the Psalms that David penned were a result of the consistent input from "governor Saul." To me, Saul appeared to be an obstacle that stood in the way of David as he made the ascent; now I see Saul as the "governor" who controlled the speed with which David ascended the throne. God knew the time it would require for David's character to be shaped into a servant-leader and shepherd of Israel. Saul was used by God to keep David from speeding to the throne prematurely.

My New Testament hero, Paul, also had a governor that he wrote about in Second Corinthians 12:7. Paul called his governor a "thorn in the flesh." Paul even asked God to remove the governor (thorn), but God knew that the governor was for Paul's good and His glory. Paul's giftedness, revelation, and wisdom were kept in check by this governor (thorn), lest he become absurdly conceited.

My ultimate hero, Jesus, did not need a governor, but He still submitted to earthly governors as an example for me: governors such as a limited human body, an imperfect family, very inept disciples, religious leaders, and the humiliation of the cross. Jesus took the lead example in teaching us how to submit to "governors" who seem so unreasonable.

When my parents were teens, governors were put on gas pedals so parents did not have to worry about high-speed races through town. I am grateful for a heavenly Father who knows how dangerous I would be if my life did not have some type of monitoring. I am now grateful for the "governors" whom God has placed in my life—people who love me but aren't as excited as I am about my plans and pursuits.

> *Although he was a son, he learned obedience from what he suffered* (Hebrews 5:8).

REFLECTION...

____

____

____

____

____

____

____

____

____

____

SHE HAD IT ALL

Have you ever met a woman who is married to the perfect man? Maybe he looked like the perfect husband. Maybe she wanted you to think he was perfect.

Have you ever met a woman with the perfect body (sigh, groan, ugh)? She never thinks it is perfect; she can readily point to her flaw(s).

Have you ever met a woman who lives in the perfect house (parade of homes winner)? I have been in several awesome houses, but the head of the manse can always show you something that needs changing or upgrading.

Well, I know a woman who was married to the perfect man (one has lived on this planet); she had the perfect body; she lived in the perfect house. Was she content with all that God gave her? "But godliness with contentment is great gain" (1 Tim. 6:6). Was she a classic example of the lady of contentment? No, she actually believed a lie that God had not provided for all her needs. I know you have already guessed the name of the woman I am referring to—and you are absolutely right—Eve.

Eve believed a lie concerning God's provision for all she needed as a woman. Ironically, the lie that she chose to believe cost her:

- her perfect husband
- her perfect body
- her perfect house

The descendants of Eve have often believed the lies that rob them of things more valuable than a perfect husband, a perfect body, or a perfect house. All of Eve's daughters have believed lies that have robbed them of the security of knowing that they are:

- deeply loved

- fully pleasing
- totally forgiven
- accepted and complete in Christ

(Read Robert McGee's *Search for Significance*, a must for any daughter of Eve who lacks the above security.)

Eve lost what we will never have, but we can have so much more than the liar wants us to believe. We will "lack no good thing" when we understand what it is to fear and seek the Lord.

> *Fear the LORD, you his saints, for those who fear him lack nothing. The lions may grow weak and hungry, but those who seek the LORD lack no good thing* (Psalm 34:9-10).

Reflection...

A MAN'S TRIP THROUGH THE BIRTH CANAL

Apart from Adam, every man enters the world through a woman's birth canal. Now that is not a brilliant revelation—but today the Lord showed me that a man enters the world of emotional freedom through the woman—like going back into the birth canal. Let me explain.

Time and time again, I have witnessed men dealing with their own stuff spiritually and emotionally (blindspots, generational cycles, hidden struggles) after their wives have already begun this process. Because men are visual, they watch what we do more than hear what we say (see 1 Pet. 3:1). When a woman stops focusing on her husband for her source of love, joy, peace, and wholeness, then her husband takes notice of her behavior toward her heavenly Husband (see Isa. 54:5).

When a woman wants her husband to be her *source* of love, joy, peace, and more, she puts immeasurable pressure on him. God never intended a man to be everything a woman needs—that is an idolatrous mentality and doesn't sit well with our heavenly Bridegroom. The more a woman discovers that Jesus is her *source*, the more she removes such pressure from her husband. Then the man can move into the birth canal for entrance into a world where he will deal with his own issues and his own baggage.

A woman is constantly looking for the best method to change her husband. All the while, her very relationship with Jesus is the most powerful method of impacting her husband. The Bible instructs a man to live with his wife with the ever-present awareness that she is a *science*. She is a "knowledge" to be studied (see 1 Pet. 3:7 KJV). A critical aspect of science is observation—as a man observes a woman dealing with "her inside stuff," he begins to get clues about the existence of "his inside stuff."

My husband is in a men's accountability group. Recently the group members discussed something they had observed (scientific) as men: a woman's liberty to talk about her "inside stuff" and a man's lack of liberty to speak about his "inside stuff." The men agreed that men, in general, are only comfortable with talking about the superficial "outside stuff" (sports, hunting, business).

I have observed God both breaking and healing the wives who are married to the men in my husband's group. As each wife deals with her own stuff, there seems to be a parallel movement on the part of her husband. One by one, I have witnessed the husbands moving (though nervously) into the "birth canal," where they are being made ready for entrance into a new world, a world where they will have to deal with their "inside stuff" and learn to be more comfortable talking with other men about the "inside stuff" (see Ps. 51:6). Is the man you love in the "birth canal" yet? What is he observing in your life concerning your dealing with your "inside stuff"? Your freedom through being complete in Christ (see Col. 2:10) is a pitocin drip to bring on labor and move him into the birth canal.

> *If any of them do not believe the word, they may be won over without words by the behavior of their wives* (1 Peter 3:1b).

Reflection...

___

___

___

___

___

___

___

___

From the School Bus Into the Arms of Jesus

The lump in my throat is so large that I can't swallow. The ache in my heart is so deep, I feel as though my breathing is labored. I can't get to sleep because I am so burdened for Rachel's mommy, a single parent holding three jobs in order to care for her four daughters.

Not even the president of the United States has a job as difficult as the role of a single parent. The single parent does not have a mate, a cabinet, a full office staff, or thousands of civil servants to help with the demands of life. Rachel's mom must face three jobs and the countless needs of four daughters—with very little help.

This struggling single mom was dealt a tragic blow that was felt not only by the Christian school her children attend, but also by our whole community. While parking her school bus, Rachel's mom accidentally ran over her youngest daughter. Rachel was killed instantly. When the story of this tragedy hit the local news, a gasp spread throughout the Christian community. It is incomprehensible how any parent can face the accidental death of a child. Yet, as I sit here writing after midnight, I know that as deep as the pain is, God's grace is equally as deep. I know from the testimony of other parents who have faced the tragic death of a child that the grace of God sustains where the mind and emotions cannot comprehend.

Rachel's mom used to be our children's bus driver; our daughter, Jessica, knew who Rachel was; Rachel's sister was in sixth grade with Jessica. Rachel, who was four years old, was the youngest of the four sisters. Our Jessica was so upset about this tragic death and asked so many questions that I could not answer...like the questions that run through each of our minds whenever we face a crisis or tragedy.

Jesus whispered something to me about little Rachel that comforted Jessica. I told Jessica that in a split second, Rachel went from the school bus into the arms of Jesus where she will be kept safe until her mom and sisters arrive in heaven, "...away from the body and at home with the Lord" (2 Cor. 5:8b).

When Rachel's daddy walked out on his wife and four girls, his abandonment sent a crushing blow to their hearts. God has taken care of this family: He has been a compensatory Father to these fatherless girls. I am praying that in this most distressing circumstance, Rachel's mom will allow her faithful and dependable heavenly Husband (see Isa. 54:5) to comfort and carry her through this numbing, breathless time in her life. The community of believers is rallying around Rachel's mom and three sisters. God's comfort and love is being delivered with "flesh on it."

For he stands at the right hand of the needy one... (Psalm 109:31).

REFLECTION...

A SNARE IN MY SOUL

Recently I watched a segment of a television program, 20/20, which focused on the physical hazards directly related to anger. For several years I have been aware of the damaging physical effect of anger: higher susceptibility to sickness and serious illnesses such as heart disease, cancer, ulcers, etc. Ironically, whenever you go to a doctor, he asks for information on your family's medical history: heart disease, cancer, and diabetes—but I have never seen "anger" on the medical form. My father died from congestive heart failure. I believe that the specific root of all his physical complications could be traced to the raging anger that pulsed throughout his life.

"Do not make friends with a hot-tempered man, do not associate with one easily angered, or you may learn his ways and get yourself ensnared" (Prov. 22:24-25). I never had a choice about living with a hot-tempered father. I never had a choice about associating with a huge clan of easily angered people. Attending family get-togethers was always another occasion for a big fight. One Thanksgiving, arguing broke out during dinner. One by one, my brothers and sisters (I'm the oldest of seven children) and their families began to leave. When the noise subsided, my husband was the only one remaining at the table. I grew up with the mind-set that anger was an unavoidable daily reality.

When I became a Christian, I realized that I had a "snare" in my soul. I often cried and asked Jesus to remove my propensity toward anger (see Heb. 12:1). I realized that I had a choice to be angry or not—a choice to decide what I associated with anger. After years of studying and soul-searching, I am learning how to manage my propensity for anger. The Holy Spirit has taught me that I can be angry and not sin (see Eph. 4:26). Just repent and forgive before sunset! The Holy Spirit also gives me the power to not harm myself or others with the anger I sometimes experience. "Better a patient man than a warrior, a man who controls his temper than one who takes a city" (Prov. 16:32). Controlling anger is not merely "pushing it underground," a process that looks like control but will allow anger to erupt later in bitterness and/or depression.

Anger has many sources; many substances fuel its fire. I was not only raised in an angry family, but I am also living in an angry nation. My heart aches for the wounded hearts hovering behind so much of the anger that I see daily. I am committed to controlling my anger by looking honestly at my own wounded heart and at the fuel such woundedness provides. As Jesus heals my wounded heart, my anger is decreasing. My soul is not so ensnared.

> *Too long have I lived among those who hate peace. I am a man of peace; but when I speak, they are for war* (Psalm 120:6-7).

Reflection...

HE CAN GIVE A SONG IN HELL

Have you ever felt proud of God? Have you ever cheered for something awesome He did: "Way to go, God!" Recently, I learned about something that God did to make me so proud of the incomparable God whom I serve. A friend of ours, who went on a mission trip to the Dominican Republic with Prison Fellowship International, told us the following story:

He went to minister in a prison called "La Victoria," originally designed for 700 prisoners but now housing 4,000 men for crimes ranging from petty theft to murder. Conditions were so crowded that he literally waded through a mass of humanity. The smell was beyond the point of being overwhelming. It brought tears to his eyes, not just from the inhumanity, but also from the mixture of aromas, none of which was pleasant. The men were housed in huge, dimly lit cells that were about 20 feet by 100 feet (2,000 square feet). In each of these cells lived more than 170 men. The restroom facilities for this mass of men consisted of a small room at one end, a room with a couple of holes in the floor, and a couple of faucets. There the prisoners bathed, washed clothes, and carried out other basic necessities. Everywhere, men were cooking over primitive hot plates to supplement their daily allowance of a dime's worth of food given by the prison at the two feedings per day.

As our friend moved through this inhumane, decrepit prison, he began to hear loud a cappella singing of Christian songs. He came upon the dining hall/chapel where 300 or more men were singing songs of praise. In this horrible circumstance, God was able to develop unbridled spiritual enthusiasm in the hearts of men. When our friend preached, the men cheered for God. When he had finished preaching, the men all cried out in Spanish—a deafening unison: "Jesus Christ has set me free! Jesus Christ has set me free!"

This story just knocked my socks off. I was overwhelmed to think about singing praise in such a despicable place. I was stunned that men, while in such a dreadful prison, could declare freedom in Jesus. God was able to give hope, passion, and praise in a place as hopeless as "hell." I am so proud of my heavenly Father who can supernaturally put a song in the heart of people who live in the most putrid sewer. "...He leads forth the prisoners with singing..." (Ps. 68:6). I am so proud of my heavenly Father who can give strength and hope in the unspeakable situations of life. Our God is incomparable, and throughout the world He is proving this reality. It is my privilege to be one of His witnesses to His "numero uno" status in the universe.

> *...Did I not proclaim this and foretell it long ago? You are my witnesses. Is there any God besides me? No, there is no other Rock; I know not one* (Isaiah 44:8).

Reflection...

I DO NOT WANT TO BE BURIED WITH MOSES

Do you become angry when things do not go the way you planned? Do you become frustrated when other people are upset because you cannot fix what is wrong? I used to assume that my anger was just a manifestation of the sin that so easily trips me up. Then God used a chapter in the Book of Numbers to shed some new light on my aggravation and frustration with life, circumstances, and people.

Moses and Aaron were faced with an angry crowd (more than two million strong) who were upset by a life-threatening situation: no water for so many in the middle of the desert. The people wanted Moses and Aaron to tell them what they planned to do about the need for an ocean of water in the middle of the desert. Moses and Aaron took this enormous need to God, who told them exactly what to do: "...Speak to that rock before their eyes and it will pour out its water..." (Num. 20:8).

As Moses and Aaron gathered the grumbling people in front of the rock, I believe that Moses moved from faith in God to anger with the complaining crowd. Instead of speaking to the rock, Moses struck the rock in anger (see Num. 20:11). Moses' anger with the rebellious, grumbling people robbed him of the trust that he had demonstrated in the presence of Pharaoh and at the edge of the Red Sea. God saw Moses' anger with the people as a missed opportunity to honor God in front of the people. "...Because you did not trust in me enough to honor me as holy in the sight of the Israelites, you will not bring this community into the land I give them" (Num. 20:12).

That passage just broke my heart because I am sure that Moses knew what it was to trust, but he was blinded by his anger with the people. Instead of focusing on God and the rock, Moses took his eyes off the glory of God and focused on the murmuring community he was leading. The people's problem with trusting the God of Israel became Moses' problem.

For several years, whenever I would read about Moses' anger and the consequence—not entering the Promised Land—I would grieve that my anger, like that of Moses, would cost me the "promised land." (I don't mean heaven, but my inheritance in Jesus.) This year, when I read through this passage, I saw that Moses' anger was a symptom of his lack of trust. I would never have correlated my anger with circumstances or people as a deeper root issue: a lack of trust in a sovereign God. For years I have felt sorry for Moses because I felt that his frustration and anger with a rebellious group of people were justified. I felt that Moses was frustrated with a people who could doubt after witnessing the parting of the Red Sea.

Then God showed me that even Moses, a man of great faith (see Heb. 11:23-29), struggled with trusting God, which was manifested through his anger. Whenever I am angry, I consider not only the person or circumstance, but also the extent to which I am failing to trust God. I do not want my tombstone in Moab (see Deut. 34:1,5-6).

> *This is because both of you broke faith with me in the presence of the Israelites...* (Deuteronomy 32:51).

REFLECTION...

GET BEHIND ME, GOD

Who would ever say to God, "Get behind me, please"? If anything, we want to be following closely behind God. Can we thrust God behind our backs? What could possibly place God behind us rather than in front of us? The key to such bizarre behavior is in the area of idolatry. "You have done more evil than all who lived before you. You have made for yourself other gods, idols…you have provoked me to anger and *thrust me behind your back*" (1 Kings 14:9). Now you are breathing easier because you know you are not into the worship of idols.

Let's look a little closer at the word *idol*. The last verse in First John is a warning about Christians "keeping themselves from idols" (see 1 Jn. 5:21). That verse has always intrigued me because I know it is not just a cultural warning for the first-century believer. I have learned that an idol is any substitute for Jesus at the center of my life. I know that an idol is anyone (or anything) from whom (or which) I try to draw love, joy, and peace.

Here's a little "check for idols" in your life. Can you think of any person or thing that has robbed you of your peace and/or joy this week? We constantly hear the remark, "________ just ruined my whole day!" You can fill that blank in with a person's name or the name of a material possession. You may fill the blank in with your car breaking down, or a phone call from your mother-in-law. A person is an idol in your life when that person can ruin your day. A possession is an idol in your life when its damage or loss can rob you of your peace and joy.

Keeping myself from idols simply means considering the place and power that I give to certain people and things in my life. For example, if my husband can ruin my day and rob me of peace and joy—then he has moved from a mate's proper place in my life to God's place. My husband is now in front, and

God is thrust behind me. When a child can ruin my day, then that child has moved from a special place in my world to the "center" of my world. That is a place for only Jesus (see 2 Kings 17:41).

My husband, my children, my mother, my mother-in-law, my ministry...and the list goes on...each of these can remain in their proper place in my life or they can shift to God's place. Jeff VanVonderen calls this shift an "impulse towards idolatry." People and things can cause us pain, but if the pain controls us and keeps us from God's peace, then we have given this person or thing God's place in our lives.

The saddest aspect of this "impulse towards idolatry" is what we forfeit when we cling to people and things more than we cling to God. Ironically, when we are in pain, we turn to people and things to comfort us; consequently, we forfeit God's grace—our greatest comfort—which becomes sacrificed by our idolatrous choice.

> *Those who cling to worthless idols forfeit the grace that could be theirs* (Jonah 2:8).

REFLECTION...

____

____

____

____

____

____

____

____

____

____

EVERYTHING SAID WAS WISE AND HELPFUL

One verse made me slam on my brakes this morning. It described Samuel's verbal ministry.

"As Samuel grew up, the Lord was with him, and everything Samuel said was wise and helpful" (1 Sam 3:19 NLT).

What powerful six words: "Everything said was wise and helpful." This became the cry of my heart for today. What did Samuel do that made his words so effective in helping people? Jesus led me to a previous passage: "...Speak, LORD, for your servant is listening..." (1 Sam 3:9).

In Hebrew, listening is *sama*—this refers to "undivided attention." I ponder the impact of a person giving God this kind of attention. The Holy Spirit brought to my remembrance another prophet who gave God "undivided attention."

> *The Sovereign LORD has given me an instructed tongue, to know the word that sustains the weary. He wakens me morning by morning, wakens my ear to listen [sama] like one being taught* (Isaiah 50:4).

Hooray, Isaiah knew the key to "wise and helpful words," listening morning by morning to the Sovereign Lord's instruction. The Hebrew word for "sustain" is used only once in the Old Testament. "Sustain" means "to hasten to help support." Now it's getting intense—why? Because I know that so often Christians rush to provide answers to suffering and trials, and in their rush they offer utter nonsense to those in pain. In this light, our words are not helpful and our words hit the ground where they rot.

First Samuel 3:19 says, "The LORD was with Samuel as he grew up, and he let none of his words fall to the ground." Yikes—words that fall to the ground. What is usually on the ground? Rotting vegetation, roadkill, and trash. This question echoed in my mind: What are rotten words? What words belong in the trash rather than in a gift package sent to a suffering person?

You won't believe what the Holy Spirit showed me next: "Do not let any *unwholesome talk* come out of your mouths, but only what is helpful for building others up according to their needs, that it may *benefit* those who listen" (Eph 4:29).

Well, knock me off my chair already.

Unwholesome talk—the word for "unwholesome" in Greek means "rot/decay." Remember the words of Samuel that the Lord kept from falling to the ground. If we are to avoid *unwholesome* words pouring out of our mouths in the presence of the needy, we need to give the Lord our "undivided attention." I used to say of my son: "If I don't have his eyes (looking at mine), I don't have his ears." If our eyes are not focused on the truth of God's Word, we will be vulnerable to "rushing to say things that are not beneficial to those who are listening."

The word for "building others up" in Greek implies "spiritual profit." Is it spiritually profitable for people to hear what you are getting ready to say? What does an undivided listener have to offer a needy listener? Benefit! The word for "benefit" in Greek is *charis*, which means "grace, a gift causing delight in the recipient." Do our words cause delight in the recipient? Are they a gift to the listener? Do our words build up or tear down? The Hebrew word for "fall" (words fall to the ground) refers to "being brought down, a violent fall".

How ironic that for years I have heard youth leaders use Ephesians 4:29 to keep teens from saying "cuss words." Instead, these leaders could have challenged teens to consider that their conversations have the power to be "a gift" or to be "roadkill rot."

One last thought—Isaiah remarked about the sovereign Lord being his instructor. What is so impressive about Isaiah referring to God's sovereignty is that only a sovereign God knows what benefits the wounded heart! Without "undivided attention" on God's sovereign understanding, we are incapable of being helpful encouragers.

> *Timely advice is as lovely as golden apples in a silver basket* (Proverbs 25:11 NLT).

REFLECTION...

AILING HEART, ANGRY MOUTH

Have you ever seen a simple discussion turn into a heated argument and said to yourself, "What was that really about?" Have you ever said something hateful, and your immediate response was, "Where did that come from?" What is fueling such harsh remarks and argumentative statements? "For out of the overflow of the heart the mouth speaks" (Matt. 12:34b). How disappointing to realize that harsh remarks and argumentative attitudes are the "overflow" of my heart, mind, will, and emotion!

In Luke 2:50-51, Jesus made some remarks that his parents did not understand, and his mother pondered them in her heart for years. The remarks that she pondered were words of such deep wisdom that she would only comprehend them when Jesus was a man. As a child, I heard remarks that I did not understand. I, too, pondered them in my heart for years. The remarks were not full of wisdom but were very harsh and deeply painful. Now, as an adult, I understand the impact of the harsh words that I heard so regularly. My heart's overflow is too often a painful reminder of what I stored there years ago. The sarcastic and critical things I heard as a child, I kept hidden in my heart; I was often angered by what I did understand. Such anger in my young heart took root to produce a debating, argumentative teenager and young adult.

I have struggled for many years with anger and harsh remarks. Only in the last ten years have I understood the correlation of the angry remarks and an "ailing" (sick) heart. I found a verse in the Book of Job that refers to the anger that flows from an ailing heart. I looked up the Hebrew word for "ailing," and it means "pressed to pungent, to irritate."

Talk about a searchlight being turned on in my soul! Suddenly I understood the source of the angry overflow: past hurt feelings of abuse, injustice, criticism, and rejection—all of these have been pressing on my heart, and the overflow has been pungent. Years of stored feelings of pain have fermented in a very angry, sick heart. By God's grace, I have been given the strength to look at the issues that I have pondered over the years. Through forgiving so many who contributed to the "pungent overflow," my ailing heart is getting better. My angry mouth and argumentative attitude are becoming more of a distant memory than a daily occurrence.

The next time you are with an argumentative person, pray for insight into the things that have been pressing on that person's heart to cause such an angry overflow. The past is not an excuse for our present anger, but it can give us clues to deal with the pungent storage that is a constant fuel line to an angry, argumentative attitude. Knowing what is in the storage areas of one's heart allows one to confront those things that supply the crushing remarks spilling out of an ailing heart through angry lips.

What ails you that you keep on arguing? (Job 16:3b)

REFLECTION...

IF GOD IS FOR ME, WHO CAN BE AGAINST ME?

Have you ever been criticized so harshly that the pain knocked the breath right out of you? I lived in a household where this was a part of the daily schedule! One day a godly woman said to me, "Whenever you are criticized, consider the source and that will help you monitor your reaction." I thought a long time about the expression, "consider the source," and I became so excited about this *fact*: God, who knows me through and through, still chose me for Himself.

God's foreknowledge did not keep Him from choosing a sinner like me. Without foreknowledge, people make some serious mistakes—but God, who is all-knowing, never makes mistakes and is never caught off guard. This all-knowing God did not choose against me, but for me.

Whenever I am criticized, I first ask the Lord to show me any aspect of the criticism that may be truth, so I can repent and let Jesus transform that blind spot in my life. When the criticism contradicts something that Jesus says about me, I choose to value Jesus' opinion rather than people's opinions. Whatever people say about me, I accept but lay the comments alongside Jesus' biographical sketch of me—that is where I live, rest, and have confidence. Jesus' biographical sketch for one of His girls would read something like this:

- She is chosen and dearly loved by *Me* (see 1 Thess. 1:4; Col. 3:12).
- She is a child of *Mine*, part of *My* family (see Rom. 8:15-16).
- She is free to call *Me* "Daddy" (see Gal. 4:6).
- She was on *My* mind before I spoke the world into existence (see 2 Tim. 1:9).

- She is a one of a kind, custom designed by *Me* (see Eph. 2:10).
- She is getting better with every passing moment (see 2 Cor. 5:17).
- She is part of a royal calling and responsibility (see 1 Pet. 2:9-10).
- She is an heir of an unshakable kingdom (see Gal. 4:6-7; Heb. 12:28).
- She is aware of her enemy, but is dauntless (see 1 Pet. 5:8).

The next time someone speaks to you in a harsh and critical manner, just pause and think: *Excuse me, do you know with whom you are speaking?* That thought always puts a smile on my face, which puzzles the one who would slay me verbally.

Why do we continue to allow people's rejection to control us more than the acceptance that we have received from God Almighty through Jesus???

> *In face of all this, what is there left to say? If God is for us, who can be against us?* (Romans 8:31 Phillips)

Reflection...

Are You Fighting Someone Else's Battle?

How often I have fallen into bed totally exhausted by a day full of so many demands, so many voices, and so many needy people! Too often I have been drained because I fought battles that were not mine. I had listened to a voice full of pain and assumed that I needed to do something. I had heard about a crisis situation and immediately considered how I would squeeze this need into my full schedule. Because of my tendency to fall prey to the "messiah complex," I have too often charged into a battle that was not even in my territory.

This tendency is not necessarily a lack of spirituality; one of the greatest kings of Judah died because he rushed out to fight a battle that was not his. It is said of King Josiah: "As long as he lived, [he] did not fail to follow the LORD" (see 2 Chron. 34:2,33). So when he charged into battle against the king of Egypt, Josiah was a righteous king. Yet, his spirituality did not keep him from the deception of a stubborn "messiah complex." King Neco sent a messenger to tell Josiah that this was not a battle between King Neco and King Josiah—who totally disregarded the warning, disguised himself, and charged into battle where he was mortally wounded.

Josiah used a disguise to get into someone else's battle. I, too, have used several disguises to "justify" my involvement in conflicts that are not mine. Maybe you have some of the same disguises in your closet:

- "Selfless Caring Christian"
- "Sensitive Servant"
- "Sacrificing Saint"
- "Sincere Counselor"
- "Strong Rescuer"

These names are sometimes disguises for an exhausted approval addict who is trapped into performing by spiritual peer pressure. Often I have felt that because the need was presented to me, it was an automatic "go" for me to jump into my chariot and charge forth to do battle for God. When I am fighting a battle that is not mine, I, like Josiah, will be wounded by arrows not intended for me. Fighting battles that are not mine is like being a masochist—wounding myself through stubborn over-involvement.

Lord, I do not want to die prematurely (ministry-wise through burnout) from engaging in battles that are not mine! Help me to judge each demand, each cry for help, and each desperate need on the basis of whether or not it is part of Your "yoke" that is easy and Your "burden" that is light.

> *After all this, when Josiah had set the temple in order, Neco king of Egypt went up to fight at Carchemish on the Euphrates, and Josiah marched out to meet him in battle. But Neco sent messengers to him, saying, "What quarrel is there between you and me, O king of Judah?"* (2 Chronicles 35:20-21a)

REFLECTION...

____

____

____

____

____

____

____

____

____

____

A WORSHIPER SEDUCED

A groundbreaking book has raised my antennae about a believer's capacity for seduction. The book is Beth Moore's *When Godly People Do Ungodly Things: Arming Yourself in the Age of Seduction.*

This morning while studying, I came across a passage that just shouted "seduction alert!" The passage is Numbers 3:4a NLT: "But Nadab and Abihu died in the LORD's presence in the wilderness of Sinai when they burned before the LORD a different kind of fire than he had commanded."

This is a familiar story to many, but its significance might escape the reader. I was inspired to look up the names Nadab and Abihu in Hebrew. It is breathtaking how the meanings of names illuminate and unveil the rich message within a passage of scripture. Nadab means "spontaneous volunteer." Abihu means "worshiper of God."

Here you have Nadab, a "hand-waving, pick-me, enthusiastic volunteer" and his brother Abihu, the "God worshiper." However, they died because they disobeyed God. How do such prime candidates for the priesthood make such a foolish choice? Just like Eve (see 2 Cor. 11:3), they were seduced by the dragon of all lies. This fire-breathing evil one is prowling our earth with the intent to exact revenge on God by wreaking havoc on His children.

My burden today is that I will never think for one moment that I have immunization against making a foolish, costly choice (see 1 Cor. 10:12). I have been an "enthusiastic, spontaneous volunteer" since I met Jesus and I am reminded of the price tag of disobedience. I am even more sensitive to the subtle seduction that can enter the life of a spontaneous volunteer and worshiper of God. My heart's cry for myself and for you is that we would finish well the race set before us and that not one of us would become a statistical casualty.

Therefore I do not run like a man running aimlessly; I do not fight like a man beating the air. No, I beat my body and make it my slave so that after I have preached to others, I will not be disqualified for the prize (1 Corinthians 9:26,27).

REFLECTION...

RELYING ON A PIERCING SPLINTER

When you are hit with a tragedy/disappointment, who do you call first? Do you call your husband, or maybe your mom, or even your prayer partner? I call all three—they are like a human trinity to me. It is wonderful to have people who love you and will stand by you in a crisis. The limitation of this earthly trinity is captured in a phrase my first pastor used to say to us, "Rely upon people, and you can only get what people have to give. Rely upon God, and you get all He has to give." My earthly trinity becomes a *piercing splinter* when I rely totally upon it and neglect my heavenly Trinity.

Israel had the support of the heavenly Commander-in-Chief, but would often turn to earthly generals for necessary support. "Look now, you are depending on Egypt, that splintered reed of a staff, which pierces a man's hand and wounds him if he leans on it! Such is Pharaoh king of Egypt to all who depend on him" (Isa. 36:6). The armies of Egypt were awesome and intimidating and would appear strong and reliable to the naked eye. God refers to this army as a "reed and piercing splinter."

God knows that the earthly people and things that we rely upon ultimately wound us. God has known for years how much I want to totally rely upon Him, so He has permitted several difficult circumstances to invade my life and test whom I would rely upon—the strong arm of my earthly trinity or the omnipotent arm of my heavenly Trinity.

I can look back over the years and see the people whom I would rely totally upon rather than Jesus. Very often these people are a reminder to me of my disobedience of trusting people more than God. Israel had this reminder in the very nation of Egypt, "Egypt will no longer be a source of confidence for the people of Israel but will be a reminder of their sin in turning to her for help" (Ezek. 29:16a). Just think: Egypt, a nation once giving Israel confidence when they were allies, eventually became a memorial to Israel's disobedience. At one time Egypt put a cocky grin of confidence on Israel's face; then she put on a face of shame.

The next time you face a crisis, consider carefully whom you are going to rely upon—the piercing splinter of people or the *One who was pierced* so that you and I can rely on Him. Relying on Jesus turns me toward Him; relying on people turns me away from Him.

> *"Cursed is the one who trusts in man, who depends on flesh for his strength and whose heart turns away from the LORD. He will be like a bush in the wastelands; he will not see prosperity when it comes. He will dwell in the parched places of the desert, in a salt land where no one lives"* (Jeremiah 17:5-6).

Reflection...

The Abundantly Blessed Wrestler

Who is the abundantly blessed wrestler?

Many of you would immediately think of Jacob wrestling with God in Gen. 32:28: "Your name will no longer be Jacob, but Israel, because you have struggled with God and with men and have overcome." Jacob was blessed after struggling and wrestling with God and man.

Have you been struggling with God or men recently? I have. This morning in Deuteronomy 33:23 (NLT) I found a nugget that I couldn't wait to research and then share with those I love. "Moses said this about the tribe of Naphtali: 'Oh Naphtali, you are rich in favor and full of the LORD's blessings; may you possess the west and the south.'" Immediately I wondered: "Why was Naphtali so rich in favor and full of blessings?"

Here are the Hebrew interpretations:

- "Rich in favor" means that a superior is gracious and kind in reacting to an inferior; the superior is taking delight and pleasure in this servant!
- "Full of the Lord's blessings" means the completion of something that was unfinished and the filling of something that was empty....

Do you need the completion of something that is unfinished?

Do you need the filling of something that is empty?

Now prepare for takeoff!

Naphtali means "wrestling and struggling." If you've been struggling and wrestling, you are a likely candidate for God's favor and full blessing of completion of what is yet unfinished in your life. The struggle is part of the path to completion. The wrestling match does not mean you have missed the blessing; the wrestling match is an aspect *of* the blessing—like a frame around a masterpiece.

Like Jacob and Naphtali—to wrestle with God or men or circumstances is a blessed wrestling event. It's a time when you and I remember that our superior, incomparable God is pleased with us in Christ and He is going to complete the good work He has begun in each of us. God is going to use our wrestling and struggling to continue to sanctify us through and through.

> *For our struggle is not against flesh and blood, but against the rulers, against the authorities, against the powers of this dark world and against the spiritual forces of evil in the heavenly realms.* (Ephesians 6:12).

REFLECTION...

NO ACCELERATED GROWTH COURSES

When I was young, I wanted results without having to sweat. Can't I just take a pill to change? I wanted to learn in a week what others had learned in a lifetime. I was sure that I could take some accelerated course for spiritual growth. I understood that salvation cost me nothing and discipleship would cost me everything. But I was convinced (proof of my immaturity) that I could appropriate the wisdom of the ancients without having some wrinkles and gray hair. I even found a verse to prooftext my naive thinking: "I understand more than the ancients, because I keep thy precepts" (Ps. 119:100 KJV). Too often for me, "Ps." did not stand for the Psalms but for a "pretty silly" child of God.

Then I discovered that my desire for:

- "a quick fix"
- "an instant spiritual depth"
- "an accelerated growth process"

was a typical sign not only of being immature, but also of being *human.*

In Jeremiah chapters 28 and 29, the Jews were in exile among the Babylonians and they wanted to know how long their lesson was going to take? A false prophet, Hananiah, told the people that God was going to break this yoke in two years (see Jer. 28:11). The people were pleased with his false prophecy because they were in a hurry to return to their homeland. The people couldn't bear the thought of prolonged captivity so they were open to any quick fix for their struggle.

When Jeremiah prophesied that their learning process or discipline was going to take 70 years (see Jer. 29:10), can you guess whom they wanted to believe? Ironically, one of the most popular verses in Jeremiah follows the verse declaring that the people would be part of a 70-year growth process. God's promises are for us whether we are in captivity or the "promised land." Growing spiritually is a lifelong process. God's hope and peace are not only available when we are grown, but also for the entire growth process.

Are you tempted to want to believe a "Hananiah" concerning an accelerated escape from frustrating spiritual immaturity? Or do you know that spiritual growth is a lifetime process that climaxes in heaven? That is why it is called the "Christian life" rather than the "Christian day" or the "Christian moment."

In high school I ran away to a commune in Fresno, California, in search of this "accelerated spiritual depth," and all I received were hysterical parents and a visit from the police. The next time someone tells you about a program/formula for "accelerated spiritual growth," just say, "No thank you, Hananiah."

The reply to you will be: "Who?"

And you can respond, "Oh, it's an inside joke!"

> *"For I know the plans I have for you," declares the LORD, "plans to prosper you and not to harm you, plans to give you hope and a future"* (Jeremiah 29:11).

REFLECTION...

____

____

____

____

____

____

____

SINNING IN THE FACE OF GOD'S GOODNESS

Because of the spiritual abuse that takes place in Christian circles, I sometimes hesitate to share what I have learned from God's Word because I do not want to wound the brokenhearted with strong teachings that may feel abrasive. Now that I have expressed my reservation, I want to share what Jesus showed me on June 20, 1993.

As I was reading Second Samuel, I came upon the passage that records Nathan's confrontation of David's sins of adultery and murder (see 2 Sam.12). Through the prophet, God asked David how he could sin in the face of His goodness. "I gave your master's house to you, and your master's wives into your arms. I gave you the house of Israel and Judah. *And if all this had been too little, I would have given you even more"* (2 Sam. 12:8). How much more could God have given David to keep him from sinning against Him? How much more could God have given Adam and Eve to keep them from sinning in the face of His goodness?

As I grieved about the freedom that God's kids feel while they sin in the face of His goodness, God reminded me of one of His children who actually resisted sexual temptation by using the goodness of God as an effective chastity belt. Joseph resisted Potipher's wife's charming seduction by referring to the incomprehensible choice of sinning against a God who had been so good to him (see Gen. 39). Ironically, Joseph resisted the sin of adultery and found himself in prison. David surrendered to the sin of adultery and continued to live in the palace. Of course, both men ultimately reaped what they sowed—Joseph went from prison to the palace, and David was driven from the palace by his own son, Absalom.

Ultimately, God saw David's sin as despising Him and His Word (see 2 Sam. 12:8-9). "Despising" seems so strong a term, but I decided that, within the context of God's abundant blessings on David, to sin in the face of such abundance is to choose to despise the Giver. God's goodness should be an impetus for obedience, not a permissive gesture to indulge oneself. How amazing to think that God's goodness is further manifested as He forgives the one who repents of despising God's Word and Person (see Ps. 51)!

Joseph resisted adultery in the context of God's goodness; David committed adultery in the context of God's goodness. The choice is ours daily. May we follow Joseph's example of resisting sin because of the context of God's goodness to us.

> *No one is greater in this house than I am. My master has withheld nothing from me except you, because you are his wife. How then could I do such a wicked thing and sin against God?* (Genesis 39:9)

REFLECTION...

___

___

___

___

___

___

___

___

___

___

___

___

MINING FOR CONCEALED JEWELS

I was talking on the telephone with the wife of a retired ballplayer. She remarked about my knowledge of the Old Testament and said the Old Testament has always been a place where one could get too easily bogged down. So she avoided it and remained in the New Testament. My first mentor taught me that I would only understand the New Testament when I had learned the Old Testament, especially the first five books (The Pentateuch). As a teenager, I studied the Old Testament with adults who were sometimes twice my age. I loved the New Testament and couldn't bear the thought that I was merely skimming the truth because I didn't know the Old Testament.

An even more powerful impetus for learning the Old Testament came when I read what the apostle Paul considered a bonus for the believer—words hidden in the Old Testament. "For all those words which were written long ago are meant to teach us today; so that we may be encouraged to endure and to go on hoping in our own time" (Rom. 15:4 Phillips). God is able to inspire men and women to endure the most horrible circumstances. He can give encouragement during the darkest hour—He pumps this inspiration into our souls through the many lines written so long ago. To neglect the Old Testament is to neglect the bonus of encouragement, endurance, and loyalty that our Christian life requires in such a cynical, painful world.

One of the biggest bonuses I have gained by reading the Old Testament is finding out that the troubling things I see human beings doing are not new for this generation. The self-consumptive American way is not new, any more than the homosexual movement is; "there is nothing new under the sun" (Ecc. 1:9). Since the beginning of time, men have done what was right in their own eyes (see Judg. 21:25 KJV), regardless of the consequences.

I have a friend who stopped at one of those "tourist mining areas." For $15 she was able to go mining for a stone. She left with an eight-carat pink stone that she figured must be worth at least the $15 admission fee. She discovered through a jeweler that her stone was worth $800. She was thrilled to mine for a precious stone whose value was concealed to both the owner of the mine and the one mining. Her experience in that California mining site parallels the success one can have when one goes digging around in the Old Testament. The Old Testament is not only a gold mine, but also a deep shaft full of many precious stones. Are you searching for comfort, hope, wisdom, truth, direction, and encouragement? These, and more, are waiting for you to search and discover what the glory of God has concealed—concealed only to those who have not ever tried mining for these jewels. Just as man has mined for wealth, we as believers can mine for eternal riches that are ours.

> *It is the glory of God to conceal a matter; to search out a matter is the glory of kings* (Proverbs 25:2).

REFLECTION...

"GOOD" BAD EXAMPLES

We are told that if we do not learn from history, we may repeat it. I have always been receptive to learning from history, especially from the many "good" bad examples. I have witnessed several parents' mistakes that have resulted in much pain for their children. These "good" bad examples have been a good guide for me as a mother. I have also seen the mistakes made by many married couples, and their bad examples have been good for me as a willing learner who wants a marriage that will go the distance.

Since there is nothing new under the sun (see Ecc. 1:9), and we always reap what we sow even under grace—then why are we not learning from so many of the "good" bad examples in the Word? I believe that God allowed the mistakes of men to be recorded to give us a warning—to help us learn from these "good" bad examples that are grace to me.

> *Now in these events our ancestors stand as examples to us, warning us not to crave after evil things as they did. Nor are you to worship false gods as they did...Now these things which happened to our ancestors are illustrations of the way in which God works, and they were written down to be a warning to us who are living in the final days of the present order* (1 Corinthians 10:6-11 Phillips).

One of my biblical ancestors has been a very "good" bad example. The consequences he faced after his devastating choice have been a most potent warning to me as a wife, mother, and woman after God's own heart. David made a choice to commit adultery and murder; his children paid for the consequences of his sin. There were times in the early years of my marriage when it might have seemed easier to quit and leave my husband, but David's "good" bad example was such a warning that was ever present in my mind. I knew that committing adultery carries too high a price tag—whether you are a king or a mere maid.

I know a parent who made the choice that David did with Bathsheba. When I was counseling his daughter at youth camp and discovered that she had just been raped, I wept hard. She made me think of the rape of David's daughter, Tamar—who had been a virgin until she was raped, just like this teenager I was counseling. Even though people would deny any correlation between a father's choice and a child's suffering, I have never forgotten that moment with that teenage girl. Whenever I read about the rape of Tamar, I always think of the father she had and the choices he made that cost her virginity.

That story is so painful, yet I think the consequences of sinning against the light that many of us have been given is a grave reality that we often want to cover up and psychoanalyze away. I believe that disregarding the many warnings we have been given through "good" bad examples is like the illusion that we can sow but not reap because God's grace will abort any consequences (see Gal. 6:7).

> *I applied my heart to what I observed and learned a lesson from what I saw* (Proverbs 24:32).

Reflection...

____

____

____

____

____

____

____

____

THE PROSPERITY OF THE WICKED—A MIRAGE

One of the most awesome music directors who ever lived became captivated by an illusion, and this mirage resulted in a cynical attitude. I am referring to Asaph, who was appointed chief of the choir (see 1 Chron. 15:16-17). As a leader in worship and praise, he was not immune to being distracted by those who had a great deal of this life in their hands. (Of course, he did not notice that they had nothing of the other life in their hearts.) Asaph became captivated by the illusion that the wicked seem to prosper more than the righteous. Remember, a mirage is a distortion of light, and Asaph's eyes were focused on a serious distortion. Notice some of the aspects of this mirage, which he wrote about in Psalm 73. He resented these apparent blessings on the wicked:

- Beautiful bodies (verse 4)—they always have the best bodies and the most elaborate wardrobe.
- Immune to sickness (verse 5)—they always seem healthy and in peak physical condition.
- Opulent necklaces of pride (verses 6-7)—they seem to have no limit to their pride and conceit.
- Claim real estate even in heaven (verses 8-9)—they can sound as religious as the guy next door.
- Irresistible charm and charisma (verse 10)—they can wow any audience.
- No fear of God (verse 11)—they are not anxious about their spiritual condition.

- Carefree and wealthy (verse 12)—they do not seemingly have a care in the world.

This list could breed jealousy in any warm-blooded human being. All these qualities of the mirage became oppressive to Asaph as he focused his attention on them. God allowed Asaph to "drool" for awhile. Then God mercifully opened Asaph's eyes during an awesome quiet time with Him. Quiet times are great opportunities for God to draw attention to the drool that is escaping through the right side of our gaping mouths.

Job gave a powerful drool warning (see Job 24:22-24). King David also understood the tendency to drool in the presence of prosperity, and he said, "Do not be overawed when a man grows rich, when the splendor of his house increases; for he will take nothing with him…" (Ps. 49:16-17). David also knew that prosperity was not proof of God's blessing. For example, Joseph resisted sexual temptation and ended up in prison; David yielded to sexual temptation and continued living in his palace. Too often, Christians mistake material blessings as approval from God. May we stop drooling, adjust our vision, acknowledge the mirage, and proceed toward lasting riches—life in Christ.

> *When I tried to understand all this, it was oppressive to me till I entered the sanctuary of God; then I understood their final destiny* (Psalm 73:16-17).

REFLECTION…

____

____

____

____

____

SECURITY FOR OUR CHILDREN

Today at lunch, the vice president of a huge corporation in Atlanta mentioned that he has a neighbor who is a doctor, and two of his sons have committed suicide. They lived in the lap of luxury, and death was more appealing than life. Later in the day, I was driving our daughter to gymnastics, and out of the blue, she said, "Sara's (a fellow student at her school) cousin committed suicide yesterday. She was only fifteen years old." A young teenage girl, from a freshly broken home, decided that death was better than life. I started to cry. Jessica said, "Mom, why are you crying? You didn't even know Sara's cousin."

I said to Jessica, "I am crying because my heart is hurt by the things that hurt the heart of God, and I know that God's heart grieves for those who choose death rather than life." I know teen suicides are a constant reality, but my heart grieves for these teens who are too often victims of homes where there was no security for them.

Where was the fortress these teens needed? Where was their place of refuge to give them the ultimate refuge? Whatever these teens turned to for security and significance must have collapsed, and they decided that death was better than life. The security and significance that the world offers teens is like a "spider web," and it cannot support life.

The Word of God clearly states that we can offer our children a secure fortress and refuge. "He who fears the Lord has a secure fortress, and for his children it will be a refuge" (Prov. 14:26). Consider the blueprints of this security system:

- My fear of the Lord...good for my children
- My zeal for the Lord...good for my children

- My trust in the Lord...good for my children
- My tears before the Lord...good for my children
- My struggles before the Lord...good for my children
- My love for the Lord...good for my children

When my children see where I turn when I am in need of security and significance, this fortress for me will become a refuge for them. My fear and love for the Lord is the greatest security that I could ever offer our children.

> *"They will be my people, and I will be their God. I will give them singleness of heart and action, so that they will always fear me for their own good and the* ***good of their children*** *after them"* (Jeremiah 32:38-39).

Reflection...

___

___

___

___

___

___

___

___

___

___

___

___

___

TOOTHPICKS IN EYEBALLS

What a gory topic! What could I possibly be referring to? This topic refers to the pain people inflict upon themselves when they disobey an ancient principle. "But if you turn away and ally yourselves with the survivors of these nations that remain among you and if you *intermarry* with them and associate with them, then you may be sure...they will become snares and traps for you, whips on your backs and *thorns in your eyes*..." (Josh. 23:12-13). As a new Christian, I was taught this ancient principle by one of my spiritual mentors. The principle was simple: Do not date nonbelievers. I have given this same counsel to many teenage girls and single women throughout the last two decades. This counsel is not from a backwoods, legalistic mentality; it is one of the oldest principles for a "holy race" (see Ezra 9:2).

Even though this principle is clearly stated in both the Old and New Testaments, I continue to meet women (young and not so young) who think it is a rule created by religion and not a principle instituted by a loving heavenly Father. I know so many unhappy women who are married to nonbelievers. Time and time again, they admit that they had disregarded this biblical principle when they were dating. In disregarding the principle, these women inflicted whips, snares, and thorns on themselves—masochistic behavior. When a person knowingly disregards any biblical injunction, it will result in self-injury. God's principles are for our protection, but it takes faith to believe that God is not a killjoy.

I always ask women who are married to nonbelievers if anyone warned them about their choice to date and eventually marry a nonbeliever. Often they say, "No one challenged or even warned me about dating a man who didn't know Jesus personally." I am concerned that those of us who know the Lord intimately would have the courage of a Micaiah (see 2 Chron. 18). Micaiah would tell the truth even if the person ended up hating him for what he said. We need courage to speak the truth to any teenage girl or single woman who is considering dating a nonbeliever—warn her about the inevitable pain of "toothpicks in her eyes." I would rather make a gal miserable for a little while by telling her the truth than have her spend years in a miserable marriage because I didn't have a "Micaiah spirit" when it came to telling the truth.

When the great leader, Ezra, was informed about God's children intermarrying with an unholy race, his response was brutal. He tore his clothing, tore hair out of his head and beard (ouch!)—he cried and wept before the Lord. Ezra was appalled that a child of God would carelessly choose to "mingle the holy with the unholy." I, too, have grieved with women who have made this choice, but I also grieve for the casual attitude that too many women take toward a friend or an acquaintance who is dating an unbeliever (see Ezra 9:2). We cannot keep a woman/gal from disobeying God, but we can at least warn her about such masochistic behavior on her part.

Do not be yoked together with unbelievers (2 Corinthians 6:14a).

Reflection...

___

___

___

___

___

___

___

___

___

___

GET YOUR OWN MARCHING ORDERS

Once, while speaking at a singles' conference in central Florida, I heard a dramatic story of reconciliation between a daughter and her alcoholic father. When I asked details about this wonderful reconciliation, the woman (also a speaker at the conference) encouraged me to go home and "do thou likewise." I did not have an alcoholic father, but I did have a father who abused seven children. Challenged by this woman's story, I returned home with her "marching orders for 'daughter-father reconciliation.'" Well, to make a long story short, my attempt was not only futile but also nearly fatal emotionally. My attempt backfired violently, and it took me a long time to recover.

The Lord took the pain I experienced from using someone else's marching orders to teach me a very deep spiritual truth. God's ways are not a standard recipe to be duplicated by everyone. God's ways are unique and specific. What He does in one circumstance does not necessarily predict what He will do in a similar situation. God will not be boxed in by presumptuous thinking—that we can second-guess His tactics. The prophet Isaiah warned us about such presumptuous thinking (see Isa. 55:8).

King David demonstrated in Second Samuel 5:17-25 that each battle requires a separate and specific set of marching orders. In this chapter, the Philistines attacked at two different times. Even though it was the same enemy, David inquired of the Lord about the strategy he should use on each occasion. Ironically, David could have relied on his great past experience or on former marching orders, but he wisely sought God's specific marching orders for each separate time the enemy attacked. If you read this chapter, you will see that the strategy was different, even though it was the same group attacking in the same valley.

Why such a variety of marching orders? I believe it is all part of our Father's desire that we come individually to Him in our time of need. I believe that He knows that we will never learn to depend upon Him if we can find a "pre-packed, pre-digested, pre-mixed" version of intimacy with God. Of course, the Father knows how complex and subject to deception the human heart is; each emotional battlefield requires very specific "marching orders."

Please do not send people into battle with your marching orders. The next time you go into battle, check your marching orders and make sure the name stamped on them is yours and that the stamp on them is "present tense."

> *"For my thoughts are not your thoughts, neither are your ways my ways"* (Isaiah 55:8).

REFLECTION...

____

____

____

____

____

____

____

____

____

____

____

____

____

____

THE BEST MEAL YOU'VE EVER MISSED

A couple who is close to us decided to fast and pray to decide whether the wife should go back to school. They chose Monday as the designated day to seek the Lord concerning the need of $8,000 for the wife to finish her college degree. They had not told anyone about their financial needs for Stephanie's schooling. The next day, the husband's mom called and proceeded to tell her son that she and his step-father had decided on *Monday* to help with the college tuition expense. They offered to pay the full amount. Now, I do not see fasting as a "magic formula" or a "fluffy rabbit's foot," but I do believe that it is a wonderful discipline neglected by the saints of God. Let me try to explain.

One day Jesus was challenged by the "religious elite" concerning the fact that His disciples did not fast. Jesus' defense was that His disciples are not to mourn (fast) when the Bridegroom is present, *but* they will fast when the Bridegroom is taken. When I read this passage, the words of Jesus grabbed my heart and I began to search the Old and New Testaments concerning the practice of fasting. Jesus, my heavenly Bridegroom, is gone, and He said that *I would fast.*

I discovered occasions for fasting, what to do while fasting, the conditions of fasting, and those who fast. This was an extensive study, and I invite you to also get a concordance and discover the best meal you have ever missed.

I could literally write a book on the results of fasting. I have a fasting journal to record my prayer requests and the truths that God shows me from His Word on the day of fasting. I have fasted with my prayer partner on a weekly basis, and now my husband and I are fasting together regularly.

Are you a potential member of "who's who in fasting"? Here are some of our members:

- Disciples (see Mt. 9:14-15)
- Widows (see Lk. 2:36-38)
- Truth seekers (see Acts 10:30-31 KJV)
- Kings, queens, warriors, prophets, ambassadors, even children (see 2 Chron. 20:3)

Pass me my fruit juice, my Bible, and my fasting journal…why don't you join me?

> *Then John's disciples came and asked him, "How is it that we and the Pharisees fast, but your disciples do not fast?" Jesus answered, "How can the guests of the bridegroom mourn while he is with them? The time will come when the bridegroom will be taken from them; then they will fast"* (Matthew 9:14-15).

REFLECTION…

____

____

____

____

____

____

____

____

____

____

____

____

Outwitted Through Unforgiveness

Are you ever aggravated when someone cleverly outwits you? Don't you just hate when you discover that you fell for a scam? I was outwitted by an easy-going, smooth-talking police officer in Kentucky as he took 90 minutes to write up a report on a very minor accident. The outwitting continued as I talked to the insurance agent who tried to place blame where it did not belong. Well, the outwitting ended when my husband entered the picture. He challenged the one trying to outwit (intimidate) me. When Ken was finished, we received a written apology from the insurance company with the assurance that our premiums would not be affected. Ken boldly challenged the insurance company concerning their efficiency in securing the truth about the accident. (They were drawing conclusions without having consulted the witnesses.)

My heavenly Husband is ready to help whenever I am being outwitted by the father of lies (see Jn. 8:44). The outwitting ends when the lie is exposed and confronted with the Truth. For longer than I would like to admit, satan has outwitted me in the area of "unforgiveness." I had assumed that I had really forgiven a particular person because I was not trying to get revenge for the hateful things she had done. One day a young pastor's wife asked me why I did not like this particular person, and I said, "What do you mean?"

And she said, "You are always full of compliments, but you are dead silent whenever her name is mentioned." Well, I had assumed that silence was better than slander, and it was. But I still was harboring hurt feelings mingled with anger. Satan outwits me when I use "excuses" for my unforgiveness:

- Why forgive her? She'll only do it again!
- Why forgive him? He doesn't care how much I've been hurt!
- Why forgive her? I know she'll hurt me again!

- Why forgive him? He'll never say he's sorry!
- Why forgive her? She knows better than to do such a thing!

Then my wonderful heavenly Mate reminds me that unforgiveness hurts me more than it does the one I am not forgiving. When I am unforgiving, I don't even want to pray for the capacity to love this person; I'd rather ignore her. Wow, talk about being outwitted with such unloving reasoning! I have defended my unforgiveness, but I have never won in the "courts of truth." In fact, I was found guilty one day when I read Paul's strong warning to the immature saints at Corinth. Paul understood satan's greatest device—to keep the forgiven ones from forgiving. Satan wants us to live in the condition he lives in daily—"unforgiven and unforgiving." For me to believe it is acceptable to be unforgiving when I have been so forgiven, this is the ultimate outwitting. "I am most like Jesus, not when I am perfect, but when I am forgiving."

> *And what I have forgiven—if there was anything to forgive—I have forgiven in the sight of Christ for your sake, in order that Satan might not* ***outwit*** *us. For we are not unaware of his schemes* (2 Corinthians 2:10b-11).

Reflection...

____

____

____

____

____

____

____

____

____

THE BRIDE BELONGS TO THE BRIDEGROOM

For almost 30 years, I have been involved in serving the Lord. My ministry has been in the local church and also in para-church ministries. The more involved I have been, the more acquainted I have become with the grief of seeing men and women in places of leadership abuse their privileged positions and neglect the legitimate needs of God's people. After years of witnessing firsthand many incidences of spiritual abuse in churches and ministries, a root of bitterness had taken hold of my heart. As this root continued to grow, I never noticed the extent of the root system in my heart because I was always consoling myself with the parallel grief that Jeremiah, the prophet, wrote about in relation to shepherds (leaders) who do not feed their sheep (people).

One passage that painfully paralleled the biographical sketch of some pastors and ministry leaders I knew was:

> *The shepherds are senseless and do not inquire of the LORD; so they do not prosper and all their flock is scattered* (Jeremiah 10:21).

As I watched the scattering of sheep being driven away by senseless shepherds, I became more and more bitter. Then the God of all mercy and compassion sent a humble preacher to my home one day in August. I was sharing with him my grief and anger with certain spiritual leaders. He listened patiently, and then he asked, "Do you have any oil?"

My remark was, "Sure, I have some Puritan oil."

I asked him what he needed it for, and he said, "I want to pray for the sick."

My spiritual mentor had come with him, and I looked at her and said, "Is Mamie sick? Are we going to pray for her?"

And he said, "No, Jackie, you are sick!" I was embarrassed, yet I knew he was right. As he and my mentor anointed me with oil and began to pray for the uprooting of my bitterness, my heart broke and I began to confess my anger and rage for the abuse I had seen in the church and ministry. When our time of prayer was over, I felt as though I had vomited much of the toxin I had ingested. Pastor Lamb (that is really his name) told me that God would affirm the healing of my bitter heart.

The Lord knows that I always want my experiences to submit to the Word of God, and so He graciously showed me that the Bride belongs to the Bridegroom. He showed me that the Church—His Bride—is ultimately in the capable hands of her heavenly Bridegroom. He kindly, not harshly, reminded me that He is the Head of the Body of Christ. No matter how sick the body seems, the Head is not spinning out of control. Jesus also showed me that as Head of the Body of Christ, He will accomplish the work He intends even within a body that daily struggles with chronic pain and dysfunction.

The bride belongs to the bridegroom (John 3:29a).

Reflection...

BE CAREFUL WHAT YOU PRAY FOR

I have always been impressed with Hezekiah's prayer life. When he received a life-threatening letter from Sennacherib, instead of panicking, he went into the temple and spread the letter before the Lord. Then he spread himself out before the Lord in prayer. The Lord's answer to Hezekiah's prayer is recorded in Second Kings 19 and Second Chronicles 32. Talk about a heavenly terminator! The angel whom God sent annihilated all the fighting men, leaders, and officers under Sennacherib. Great answer to prayer! Quite impressive!

Sometime later, King Hezekiah became ill, and the prophet Isaiah told him to get his house in order because he was going to die. Hezekiah knew firsthand about answered prayer, so he turned his face to the wall, wept bitterly, and begged the Lord to heal him. Another impressive answer to prayer: Isaiah had not even left the palace when the Lord spoke to him and told him to go back and tell Hezekiah that he would be healed—and God was going to give him 15 additional years (see 2 Kings 20:5-6).

Now, I have always been impressed with the 15 additional years aspect of this answered prayer *until* a few summers ago when I was doing thorough research on the kings of Israel and Judah. Why I never noticed this before I do not know, but I just about flipped when I read Second Kings 21: I realized that during the 15 additional years of Hezekiah's life, a child arrived who did great evil. This evil person was Manasseh, born to Hezekiah during the 15 additional years he was given in answer to his bitter crying. Hezekiah's tears and prayers granted a life extension that gave birth to an evil offspring and heir. That child inherited his father's throne and rebuilt all the altars that his father had torn down, resurrecting all the offensive high places that his father had removed.

"Moreover, Manasseh also shed so much innocent blood that he filled Jerusalem from end to end…" (2 Kings 21:16).

Let Hezekiah's example challenge each of us to be careful what we cry and weep for. Rather than crying for our will, maybe we should copy the tears of another One who wept in prayer and follow His example rather than Hezekiah's:

> *"Father, if you are willing, take this cup from me; yet **not my will, but yours be done**" (Luke 22:42).*

Reflection…

THE SECRET OF THE ALABASTER BOX

In the days of Jesus, when a young woman reached the age of availability for marriage, her family would purchase an alabaster box for her and fill it with precious ointment. The size of the box and the value of the ointment would parallel her family's wealth. This alabaster box would be part of her dowry. When the young man came to ask for her in marriage, she would respond by taking the alabaster box and breaking it at his feet. This gesture of anointing his feet showed him honor.

One day when Jesus was eating in the house of Simon the leper, a woman came in and broke her alabaster box and poured the valuable ointment on Jesus' head (see Mk. 14:3-9). The passage in Luke 7:36-50, which refers to this event, harshly describes the woman as a woman in the city who was a sinner. Were there actually people from the city who were not sinners? Anyway, this woman found Jesus worthy of such sacrifice and honor. In fact, Jesus memorialized her gesture in Matthew 26:13: "I tell you the truth, wherever this gospel is preached throughout the world, what she has done will also be told, in memory of her." Can you imagine how angry people were that Jesus memorialized a "sinner"? Way to go, King Jesus! Your gesture of such grace is the theme of a song that is sung throughout the world by sinners—"Amazing Grace."

This broken alabaster box is full of great meaning. The woman not only anointed Jesus for his approaching burial, but she also gave her all to a heavenly Bridegroom. Yes, she was a sinner. Who isn't (see Rom. 3:23)? But this sinner had her dreams, and she wisely broke her alabaster box in the presence of the only One who can make a woman's dream come true.

What is in your alabaster box? Is it full of dreams begun as a little girl while you heard, and even "watched," fairy tales about enchanted couples who lived happily every after? Have you already broken your box at the feet of a young man who has not fulfilled your dreams and has even broken some of your dreams? Or have you been holding on tightly to your alabaster box of dreams, forever searching for a man worthy of the contents of your box? Whether your alabaster box is broken or sealed tightly shut, I encourage you to bring your box and place it at the feet of Jesus.

When you've placed your alabaster box at His feet, then you will be able to respond like Mary to a heaven-sent assignment. When Mary was asked to become pregnant while engaged to Joseph, she did not argue with the angel. Her response was that of a woman who had already broken her alabaster box at the feet of Joseph and was now ready to take her broken box and lay it at the feet of a heavenly Bridegroom.

I belong to the Lord, body and soul... (Luke 1:38, Phillips).

REFLECTION...

A BUSYBODY AND A MURDERER

Have you ever considered what a busybody and a murderer have in common? Well, God allowed Peter (are you not surprised it was Peter?!) to write about not being ashamed of suffering for doing good. Then Peter wrote the comparison of the understandable suffering for doing evil, such as, "a murderer or thief or any other kind of criminal, or even as a meddler" (1 Pet. 4:15b). I remember thinking that the word *meddler* did not fit my concept of a criminal behavior. Have you ever known anyone who has been put in jail as a convicted "meddler—busybody"? Maybe you know a certain busybody who *should* be constrained behind bars!

I decided to do a little research on the origin of the word *meddler*. I learned that meddler is taken from the word *supervise/supervisor*. So, when a woman is a busybody, that is just another word for a woman who is supervising someone else's family, business, etc. Why would that be such a crime? I realized I was onto something far deeper than a busybody mentality.

One aspect of a woman's role that is nullified by the busybody is the privileged role as "keeper of the home." That is not a role that means to "keep a woman at home." The *keeper* in Greek refers to "guarding what enters the home." A woman is free to choose what she wants to do outside her home, as long as she does not neglect the guarding of what is entering her home. Too often, when I am supervising someone else's life, family, home, business, etc., it is easy for me to neglect the guarding of my home. For me to not stand guard over my home makes our home vulnerable to all types of enemies who would enter our home and destroy my marriage and our family life. Such neglect is criminal, and it happens on a daily basis in America, even in Christian homes.

The debate concerning a Christian woman working outside her home can be settled with a simple question. How much time can you give to things outside your home and still stand guard over the things that could enter your home and harm those whom you love? With such an awesome responsibility as the keeper of our home, I am sensitive to the self-inflicted suffering that is mine when I am being a busybody. Some busybodies are bored, silly women, but many are competent, gifted women who sometimes neglect evaluating where they give their attention. Does this person, household, ministry, or task qualify under my God-given responsibilities, or is this part of a "busybody crime"? Am I supervising a marriage, a family, or even a job that is not mine? Do I let my "busybody attitude" escort me into someone else's area of responsibility?

> *They should be examples of the good life, so that the younger women may learn to love their husbands and their children, to be sensible and chaste, home-lovers, kind-hearted and willing to adapt themselves to their husbands—a* ***good advertisement*** *for the Christian faith* (Titus 2:4-5 Phillips).

REFLECTION...

ARE YOU A PAIR OF CLEATS OR A PARACLETE?

When a person in your life is hurting, are you a crushing pair of cleats or a comforting paraclete? When a woman shares her pain with you, do you further rupture her wound (like a pair of cleats) or do you help refine her faith through your comfort (paraclete)?

To be a paraclete rather than a pair of cleats, we need to be able to show genuine acceptance of the hurting person's strong feelings of disappointment and anger. Too often we react to a person's pain by giving advice rather than listening and quietly asking questions.

A paraclete will not rupture the wounded by trying to give advice prematurely. She understands that her willingness to listen encourages the healing process (see Prov. 20:5). Job's friends hurt him and angered God by giving too much inappropriate advice. Job's friends were paracletes during the first three days when they sat silently with their hurting friend. They turned into a pair of cleats when they began rambling about the *why* of Job's painful circumstances. Job's friends spoke more than 400 verses as they tried to tell him: "You shouldn't feel that way...you're just reaping what you sowed." Note God's perspective on their *advice*. "After the LORD had said these things to Job, he said to Eliphaz the Temanite, 'I am angry with you and your two friends, because you have not spoken of me what is right, as my servant Job has' " (Job 42:7).

Why do we tend to move into "panic preaching" in the presence of someone's pain? Why do we preach rather than weep with the hurting? I think I know the answer. When we, like Job's friends, come face to face with such suffering in the life of such a godly man, we panic—because we are overwhelmed that such a horrible thing can happen to someone so close to God. We start rambling and preaching in order to drown out the painful reality we are witnessing. Such panic in the presence of pain is the making of another pair of cleats. Nothing slams the door on the hurting soul faster than judgmental, panicked preaching.

The paraclete is so comforting because she has embraced her own pain. For years, people have said to me, "You seem to attract hurting people." Now I understand why. The most effective path in understanding the pain of another is through facing and embracing my own pain! J.B. Phillips captured this in his paraphrase of Second Corinthians 1:5. "Indeed, experience shows that the more we share in Christ's immeasurable suffering the more we are able to give of this encouragement." Being a paraclete to another is not only for their comfort but also for their spiritual protection.

We are indwelt by the Paraclete (Holy Spirit) so our capacity to comfort is an automatic potential. May we allow the Paraclete to use us in such a hurting world.

> *...He will give you another Counselor to be with you forever* (John 14:16).

Reflection...

____

____

____

____

____

____

____

____

____

____

____

ONE OF THE DIVINE SECRETS OF YADAH YADAH

In one sermon my pastor spoke of people being crippled by their emotions and therefore being escorted away from their destiny. As a woman, I do understand that emotions can cripple us and that we might miss a heavenly assignment because we don't feel like obeying the Lord. Everyone started laughing as my pastor went into a physical, bodily depiction of people needing "their feelings" understood. He said that if a person needs someone to listen to her feelings, he will send her to his wife or the counseling staff. He mentioned that as a "former football coach," he doesn't have the heart for such a "feeling" ministry! The audience roared and so did I. Then I pondered a question: Is a "feeling" ministry for women only?

Later as I studied for a message God has loaned me ("The Divine Secrets of the Yadah Yadah Sisterhood"), I came across some nuggets that address this "feeling ministry."

Note: The Hebrew word *yadah* means "a sense of understanding and perceiving that comes from a face-to-face/heart-to-heart knowing" (Moses with God, Deut. 34:10:"...Moses, whom the LORD knew face to face").

"God gave Solomon wisdom and exceedingly great understanding, and largeness of heart like the sand on the seashore" (1 Kings 4:29 NKJV). To lead and impact people, a person needs not only wisdom and understanding, but also largeness of heart.

This largeness of heart is reflected in the ministry of encouragement. Dr. Larry Crabb has said, "Encouragement is the kind expression that helps someone want to be a better Christian even when life is rough."

"Carry each other's *burdens*, and in this way you will fulfill the law of Christ" (Gal. 6:2). The Greek word for "burdens" means "burdened under pressure, difficulty, grief, savage-fierce weight" (all mental and emotional realities).

Are women the sole humans meant to deal with the "emotional aspects" of people's burdens? Our Lord reminded me of some verses. My soul jumped out of my chair! Consider the ultimate representative of the "feeling ministry" and this leader was not a female! "So even though Jesus was God's son, he learned obedience from the things he suffered. In this way, God qualified him as a perfect High Priest" (Heb. 5:8-9a NLT). Suffering sets the stage for the perfect leader. If you doubt for a second that Jesus escaped any emotional trials, revisit the garden and the anguish that He experienced.

"For we have not an high priest which cannot be touched with the feeling of our infirmities..." (Heb. 4:15 KJV). This is one of the first verses I learned as a young believer living in an abusive home. If I didn't believe that Jesus was touched by the feelings of my anguish, I would never have been confident enough in Him to keep following Him.

Now here is the kicker: I looked up the word "touched"—oh my goodness! The Greek word for "touched" means

- compassion
- experience pain jointly
- touched with sympathy
- having fellow-feelings

To someone who's suffering, we can offer the exceptional good news that Jesus is *touched*...by their painful feelings. Jesus is a *conjoined experience of sympathy and compassion!!!*

God called David a man after his own heart. This man was a king, a warrior, a leader, a man's man...but also *a man capable* of experiencing "pain jointly, having fellow-feeling." This man did not miss his destiny because he felt things so deeply. This man was used by God to write poetry/psalms that have comforted millions.

And look: "Praise be to the God and Father of our Lord Jesus Christ, the Father of compassion and the God of all comfort, who comforts us in all our troubles..." (2 Cor. 1:3-4). The Greek word for "compassion" means "pity, mercy, a distinguishing mark of a child of God." Our compassion for people when they are in trouble is a distinguishing mark of our relationship with the High Priest who is touched by our struggles. The Greek for "comfort" means "encouragement and strengthen; establish a believer in his faith." I love this because God does not comfort us just to erase our sadness and make us happy. God comforts us, He sends specific consolation, to purposely strengthen our faith in Him. The Greek word for "who comforts" means "comes to the side to aid with encouragement."

Note: When Jesus said He was going to send another like Himself, He called this "another" the Comforter/Counselor (John 14:26). He didn't refer to the Holy Spirit as a great leader but as a Comforter!

John Maxwell has said, "80 percent of ministry taking place in churches is done by women." Why? I know there are many factors that explain that statement, but I know without a doubt that a woman's propensity for largeness of heart is one reason God can use her so freely with so many people. I know that a woman's capacity for compassion and sympathy enables her to be "touched" by the needs of others, allowing her to cooperate more freely with the agenda of our Father.

In my 35 years of walking with Jesus, I have met a few men with largeness of heart—may their tribe increase. Personally, I praise God for all the suffering that has broken my heart, time and time again. This breaking made more room for God to accomplish my "largeness of heart." Suffering leads us to the cross, and the cross connects us to God

> *He comforts us in all our troubles so that we can comfort others.*
> (2 Corinthians 1:4 NLT).

Reflection...

A HOLY WINK FOR MOM

How would you like to see God wink at you in the middle of your busy day? That's one of the delicious goodies our Lord gave me as I was reading Numbers 6:24-26. The deeper I dug into the Hebrew words, the more good stuff I found! These verses have become my new "blessings" prayer—an alternative to the prayer of Jabez!

This passage reveals the coolest blessings that you can pray for others. In fact, verse 27 states that these blessings were exclusive to those who are God's people and God is the one who will fulfill the promises. Here are the goodies I found (my translations from the Hebrew are in parentheses):

"The LORD bless you and keep (tend you like a garden) you; (v24)

the LORD make his face shine (a splendid glow—like a face that lights up when gazing upon one that is loved(upon you and be gracious (kindness and favor for the weak [needy]) to you; (v25)

the LORD turn his face toward you (this is the ultimate "nod of affection"—like a "holy wink" in a crowd from the One who loves you) (v26a)

and give you peace (establish, set down a satisfied condition and well-being)." (v26b)

The next time you pray for someone, consider praying that he or she will allow God to tend him or her like a garden (this may involve pruning). Pray that he/she will see God's look of love and "holy wink" amid a crowded day, and that he/she will not fear weakness or neediness because God "...gives grace to the humble" (James 4:6). Finally, pray that he/she will let Jehovah-shalom be his/her supernatural peace and well-being in a less-than-perfect world.

These verses were like an early Mother's Day gift to me. I wrote them on an index card and attached it to my car visor. I hope they are a blessing to you and those you pray for. As you pray, you'll receive His "holy wink" too.

> *Know that the LORD has set apart the godly for himself; the Lord will hear when I call to him* (Psalm 4:3).

Reflection...

AUDACIOUS PRAYER REQUESTS

I am taking a great risk by recording the following thoughts; the topic is one that has disturbed my heart for such a long time. For more than two decades I have been teaching men and women, some who claim to be believers and others who are slightly interested in spiritual things. Time and time again, I have been knocked down (not knocked out) by some of the prayer requests that I have been given by certain people. I have no hesitation whatsoever about praying constantly for the men and women I am trying to minister to—but I really struggle with the audacity of some of their prayer requests.

I struggle with prayer requests from a woman who claims to love Jesus but is living with her boyfriend. I struggle with praying for women who are bearing children out of wedlock but they ask for God's blessing on their little ones. I struggle with a young woman asking me to pray that she doesn't test positive for AIDS, when I know she is still doing drugs and living with her boyfriend. I struggle with believers who can stubbornly resist God's leadership but wholeheartedly place their many prayer requests before Him. Maybe this audacity is a result of the many religions in America that serve up "a god on our terms," "a god that we don't have to obey." However, many expect their "god" to obey their requests—a "god" who does not expect anything from its followers but whose followers expect everything from their god.

While struggling with the unrestrained presumption with which people ask things from God, I came upon a people in the Old Testament who approached God with the same audacity (see Jer. 21). Here are people who are supposed to be followers of the true God, yet they attack His prophet (Jeremiah) with their tongues and pay no attention to anything he says. These same people continue to backslide further and further away from God, yet when the time of need arrives—King Nebuchadnezzar getting ready to attack their city—they call upon the very prophet they have rejected and expect him to ask God to rescue them from the enemy.

How did God respond to this stubborn, backslidden people and their cry for help? "I myself will fight against you with an outstretched hand and a mighty arm in anger and fury and great wrath" (Jer. 21:5). Lord, I do not want to encourage people to pray with such unrestrained presumption without first challenging them to turn from the sin that so easily besets them.

What does an "audacious prayer request" sound like? (Read Jeremiah 21:2.) Here is a strong warning for prayer requests from people living in stubborn disobedience.

> *If anyone turns a deaf ear to the law, even his prayers are detestable* (Proverbs 28:9).

Reflection...

God Stoops Down

Whenever a child asks for help, the adult often needs to stoop down to reach that child. You know how it is when you are carrying several packages: you drop one, and someone stoops down to pick up the package for you—such a helpful gesture.

One of the definitions of this gesture of "stooping" is "condescend/abasement". The only true God parted the heavens and stooped down to earth in the form of a man in order that mankind could know what it is like for "God to stoop down" on behalf of needy men. This abasement is willingly done on a daily basis for children of the King. Look with me at just a few of the ways that *He stoops down for His own*:

- God stoops down to sustain me (see Ps. 119:116).
- God stoops down to keep me from hurting myself (see Ps. 18:36).
- God stoops down to give me strength (see Neh. 8:10).
- God stoops down to make the way clear for me (see Ps. 18:32).
- God stoops down to train me for life's battles (see Ps. 144:1).
- God stoops down to give me light so I can walk through the darkest night (see Job 29:3).
- God stoops down to give me the capacity to scale the walls people build (see Ps. 18:29).
- God stoops in delight to rescue me (see Ps. 18:19).
- God stoops down to confide in me (see Ps. 25:14).
- God stoops down to bless me in the sight of men (Ps. 31:19).

- God stoops down to place a song in the heart of a former "slime pit dweller" (see Ps. 40:2).

- God stoops down to quiet my anxious heart with His love (see Zep. 3:17).

How awesome to think that God condescends in order not only to meet the needs of His children but also to make them great! "You stoop down to make me great" (Ps. 18:35b). As God stoops down to meet our needs, He is singing a love song over us. Have you heard the love song?

> *The LORD your God is with you, he is mighty to save. He will take great delight in you, he will quiet you with his love, he will rejoice over you with singing* (Zephaniah 3:17).

REFLECTIONS...

As president of Power to Grow Ministries, Jackie is a popular conference speaker for people of all ages and stages of life (single, married, divorced, and widowed). Her teaching style is hard-hitting, humorous, healing, and encouraging. Her teaching allows tough topics to become easier to swallow as she spices them with her savory humor and biblical style. Jackie has also coauthored Lady in Waiting, a book designed to encourage women of all ages to wait for God's best in a life mate. Jackie resides with her husband Ken in Royal Palm Beach, Florida, and they have two grown children.

Jackie is available for speaking engagements.
For more information, call or write:

Power to Grow Ministries

P.O. Box 210042

Royal Palm Beach, FL 33421-0042

(561) 795-4792

www.jackiekendall.com